DAILY READINGS FROM THE BIBLE

NEW Daylight

Edited by Shelagh Brown · *May–August 1997*

>> **The Bible Reading Fellowship**
OPENING THE BIBLE

Writers in this issue

Adrian Plass is an internationally popular writer and speaker. His book *The Unlocking: God's escape plan for frightened people* was first published by BRF in 1994. It has been translated into German, Dutch and Swedish and is now available in an updated version and on audio-cassette.

Hilary McDowell has just joined the *New Daylight* team. Her book, *Some Day I'm Going to Fly*, which tells the story of her amazing life, has a foreword by Adrian Plass and is a best seller. Hilary works as a deaconess in Belfast and exercises a ministry of reconciliation and outreach through drama, art, poetry and music.

Canon David Winter is a priest in the Diocese of Oxford. Formerly Head of Religious Broadcasting at the BBC he is a regular contributor to Thought for the Day and Prayer for the Day. A popular and prolific writer, his most recent BRF title is *Forty Days with the Messiah*. He is a General Editor of *The People's Bible Commentary*.

Rosemary Green is an internationally known speaker who is on the team of Springboard, the Archbishops' Initiative in Evangelism. She is the author of *God's Catalyst*.

Veronica Zundel (like Hilary McDowell) has recently joined the *New Daylight* team. She preaches regularly in her church and is a writer and editor.

The Reverend Marcus Maxwell is Rector of St John's, Heaton Mersey in Lancashire and the author of *Revelation* in BRF's new series *The People's Bible Commentary*.

The Reverend Shelagh Brown is the Editor of *New Daylight* and one of BRF's commissioning editors. A General Editor of *The People's Bible Commentary*, her most recent books for BRF are *Confirmed for Life* (with Bishop Gavin Reid), *Value Me* (with Phil Lawson Johnston) and *Feeding on God: discovering God through the whole of life*.

Dom Henry Wansbrough, OSB, is the Master of St Benet's Hall, Oxford, a writer, broadcaster, and General Editor of *The New Jerusalem Bible*. He is also a General Editor of *The People's Bible Commentary* and the author of *Genesis* in that series.

Several writers in this issue are contributors to the *Day by Day* series. For details see the order form on page 159.

THE BRF
Magazine

The Editor writes...

The last thing that Jesus does in the book of Acts before the Ascension is to give the disciples a promise: 'You will receive power when the Holy Spirit has come upon you: and you will be my witnesses in Jerusalem, in all Judea and Samaria, and to the ends of the earth' (Acts 1:8, NRSV).

We are realizing to our great delight that *New Daylight* is being a witness to 'the ends of the earth'. We know because of the letters you write and because of what the *New Daylight* writers tell us.

Bridget and Adrian Plass go sometimes to Australia and New Zealand. 'People keep on coming up to me', Adrian told me, 'and they say they feel they know me because they read my notes in *New Daylight*'. When Bridget and Adrian were in America the Bishop of Colorado and his wife came to their meeting. 'We came because we read *New Daylight*,' they told them.

The same goes for Rosemary Green as she speaks in countries all over the world. 'People come up to

We are realizing to our great delight that New Daylight is being a witness to 'the ends of the earth'.

me and introduce themselves because of *New Daylight*', she says, and she finds it a lovely experience. As I write Madeleine Smith is the co-ordinator of BRF in Barbados, where there are literally hundreds of readers—and Rosemary and her husband Michael are expected to be in Barbados on a speaking tour and holiday in April and May, 1997. So all the time more links are being forged and the fellowship is deepening.

'You will be my witnesses,' Christ said—and the promise is to us as well as to those first disciples. For them and for us the witnessing isn't done in our own strength but in the power of the Holy Spirit—and to witness is quite simply to tell someone what we know. As Christians we are to tell each other what we know about God-in-Christ, and we are to tell other people too: people who don't know him and who don't love him. And as we 'grow in grace and in the knowledge of God' we shall have more and more to tell about the riches of his grace and the wonder of his nature.

Each one of us is called to be a witness to Christ. To tell people what he means to us, what he's done for us, and what he does for us day by day. If we're willing, we'll meet just the people who are longing to hear what we have to tell.

'The fields are already ripe for harvest' Jesus told his disciples at the start of it all—and now there are fresh fields and a fresh harvest. Will you pray to the Lord of the harvest that he will send out fresh labourers to harvest the fields—and also offer yourself to be one of them?

If you don't know how to begin then begin by praying and asking Jesus to anoint you with his Spirit. Keep your ears open—and listen to what people say. If you really listen you'll hear how things really are for them. People desperately need to be listened to, and as you're listening, to them and to the Spirit within you, you'll know the right words to say. Or you might think of offering them something to read that seems to be just right for them.

Christian books are a wonderful way to witness to Christ—so be aware of what's available and have a selection at home that you can turn to, to give to people or to lend them. To give someone a Christian book can be a non-threatening way of introducing them to the Christian faith—and it's a very gentle form of evangelism.

Last year I was listening to Beethoven's ninth symphony and watching it on television at the same time. When it came to 'A Hymn to Joy' they ran the translation of the words at the bottom of the screen. For me one phrase shone out in letters of fire: 'Do you know your Creator, world?' Often the answer that people give is 'no'—so we can introduce them.

Each one of us is called to be a witness to Christ. To tell people what he means to us, what he's done for us, and what he does for us day by day.

Shelagh Brown

5

Richard Fisher writes...

Thank you for all your letters! During recent months we have received dozens of letters telling how and why BRF Bible reading notes are special to you—from some for whom BRF notes provided a spiritual lifeline during the Second World War, either as prisoners of war, or serving in the armed forces far from home; from some who were first introduced to the notes as a child and have read them literally for decades now; and letters from many who have found that God has spoken very clearly to them through the notes during a particular crisis or experience.

Thank you also for all your kind comments about *New Daylight* and *Guidelines*, and about *The BRF Magazine*. We are delighted that so many of you see it as a welcome addition to each issue.

Disciple

In the last issue of the *Magazine* you will have read about *Disciple*, a new initiative which is now available in the UK through a partnership between The Foundery Press and BRF. *Disciple* is a 34-session course which provides a framework for people to relate the teaching of the Bible to their discipleship today. Already many churches have sent leaders to the special three-day training seminar to learn about how to implement and teach the *Disciple* course in their churches, and *Disciple* groups are being established throughout the UK. If you

would like further details about this exciting initiative and what it might offer to your church or fellowship, send an A4 31p s.a.e. clearly marked 'Disciple' in the top left hand corner to BRF in Oxford.

Livewires and The People's Bible Commentary

These two major new resources are now available from BRF and are being very well received. We first mentioned them both in the September 1996 issue of the *Magazine* and launched them in October 1996.

Livewires is the cornerstone of our Bible reading resources for 7–10 year olds and is published under our children's imprint *Barnabas*. Look out for the Barny logo for quality children's resources from BRF. There will be 18 titles in the *Livewires* range, together providing a comprehensive introduction to the people, places and events of the Bible, along with a range of themes relating the Bible to everyday Christian life. *Livewires* is also available on subscription, and can be ordered regularly along with your *New Daylight* and *Guidelines* notes. For further details see page 157.

The People's Bible Commentary will eventually cover every book of the Bible, creating a complete library of readable commentaries which address both head and heart—deepening our understanding of the text, and enabling us to worship and pray in response to what we read. Each Bible book is divided into a number of passages and for each passage there is a double page spread of commentary and a prayer. You can therefore work through each book systematically and on a daily basis if you wish. A voucher scheme enables you to collect a voucher from each volume which counts towards further free copies. Full details are included on the last page of each commentary.

Our hope and prayer is that both these new resources will serve to draw even more readers into a deeper awareness of and relationship with God through the Bible and through prayer. If we can achieve that, then we are fulfilling the objective and vision for which BRF was brought into being 75 years ago.

BRF Representatives

As a regular reader of BRF notes you will no doubt be aware of our network of many thousands of Group Secretaries who are responsible for ordering and distributing BRF Bible reading notes to readers in their church(es). We are enormously indebted to them all for the hard work and support which they give to BRF year after year.

As we celebrate our 75th Anniversary we should like to expand this network further. If you would like details of how you could become a BRF Group Secretary in your church, or if you know someone who might be interested, please let us know.

Alongside the Group Secretary network, we are seeking to develop a network of BRF Representatives, who will promote the work of BRF as a whole (the resources, the charitable work, the vision) at a local level, building links with churches, holding book parties and events. If you are looking for a challenge and would like to become involved with BRF in this way, please contact Karen Laister here at the BRF office for further details.

Special Projects News

In the last two issues I have written of our support of ministers in Papua New Guinea, to whom we have sent BRF books. Recently a letter arrived from our main contact there, who wrote: 'We were delighted to learn of the wonderful response to the Fellowship's appeal for aid for supporting churches. We are thrilled by your news that such a large consignment of books is on its way to us... Please thank all members of the Fellowship for their support. Priests here, and Pastors the world over, must be deeply indebted to you all for providing much needed tools for Bible study, with flocks who cannot afford to buy such books as you provide.'

There is such an urgent need for those in ministry and with responsibility for teaching and preaching to be equipped properly for Bible study themselves if they are to be effective in their leadership. If you can help us to send more BRF Bible study books to those in countries like Papua New Guinea, where they either have little access to or cannot afford such resources, please do consider supporting this work. Every donation counts, no matter how large or small, and will enable us to develop this initiative further.

Romania

You will have read also in previous issues of our support for a project in Romania to help the Romanian Evangelical Society to produce a version of *New Daylight* in Romanian, combining notes translated from our own edition with those specially written by Romanian Christians themselves. This project was initially for three six-month editions, but was then extended to include a one year volume. The project has now come to an end in terms of BRF providing financial support (some £12,000 during the last three years), but we will continue to provide material from *New Daylight* for translation for the Romanian edition.

75th Anniversary

Our 75th Anniversary year continues and on page 9 you will find details of events still to come during 1997. Please do write and let us know if you are planning or have already held any special events of your own to mark this BRF milestone. And if there is anything we can do to help, do ask! For example we know of one church which is also celebrating its 75th Anniversary during the Autumn and so we are discussing plans for a joint celebration with them.

Christian Resources Exhibition

If you live within reach of Esher, Surrey, do come and visit us at the annual Christian Resources Exhibition (20–23 May 1997) at Sandown Park. Several BRF authors, including Adrian Plass, will be visiting the Exhibition and spending time with us on the BRF stand each day. BRF authors will also be involved in the extensive lecture programme. The Christian Resources Exhibition is well worth a visit—if you have never been before, why not make this year your first?

75th Anniversary Update

To remind you of what is happening and give you new information regarding events and initiatives for the remainder of the year…

Group Secretary Day

The final Group Secretary Day will take place on 13 September. If you are a Group Secretary you should already have received details of this. If you have not had these, please let us know as soon as possible.

Christian Resources Exhibitions

Come and meet BRF authors and staff, find out more about the work of the Fellowship and see the latest new publications.

20–23 May 1997
Sandown Park, Esher, Surrey

23–25 October 1997
G-MEX, Manchester.

Bible Sunday

Full details of the outline service, drawing from the Service of Thanksgiving and Rededication (which was held on 30 January), will be available in the next issue of the *Magazine*.

Author Tour

We can now announce that our author tour in October will be with Adrian Plass, whose new book will be published by BRF that month. Final details of dates and venues will be published in the next issue of the *Magazine*, but if you wish to have the information earlier, please send an A5 20p s.a.e. clearly marked 'Plass Tour' in the top left hand corner to BRF in Oxford.

Information Pack

This is still available, containing ideas and suggestions for what you might do in your own church or area to celebrate BRF's anniversary and to promote and encourage Bible reading. Contact the BRF office to request your copy.

Souvenir Brochure

This will be available to all readers of the notes during the latter part of the year and will include the story of how BRF came into being. Details of how you may obtain your copy will be included in the next issue of the *Magazine*.

Profile of The Rt Revd Patrick Harris

The Right Reverend Patrick Harris is the Bishop of Southwell and also the Chairman of the Bible Reading Fellowship's Council.

He has been married to Valerie since 1968, and they have three grown-up children. Jonathan, who is a teacher at Dean Close School; David, who works in Boots; and Rachel, who, after taking a degree in anthropology, is now doing a Post-Graduate Certificate of Education at Oxford Brookes University.

Patrick Harris spent most of his childhood in St Alban's and went to St Alban's School. After doing his two years' national service with the Royal Artillery in Germany he read law at Oxford. Before going to Keble College, Oxford, a friend asked him a question which changed the course of his life.

> *'Do your best to present yourself to God as one approved, a workman who has no need to be ashamed, rightly handling the word of truth.'*

'He challenged me as to whether God might not be calling me into the ministry,' Patrick Harris told me. 'Wham.' With the realization that God was indeed calling him, he went through the selection process and eventually did his theological training in Bristol at Clifton Theological College.

His first job was as curate to The Revd Basil Gough at St Ebbe's Church in Oxford. Then for the next seventeen years he was in Argentina, serving with the South American Missionary Society. 'I was working with the Mataco Indians', he told me, 'and I am bilingual in Mataco and in Spanish.' He still has a great interest in South American, particularly

10

Indian, culture. 'I am going back to Argentina for a week in October', he said. 'I have been a member of the South Atlantic Council which has sought to bridge-build after the Falklands War between the two countries. I will be a delegate in the Argentine–British Conference which is held annually.'

Patrick Harris likes reading—and biographies are particular favourites. 'At the moment I'm reading an exhaustive biography of Cranmer, who was a son of Nottinghamshire, by Diarmaid MacCulloch' he said, 'and another on Jorge Luis Borges, *The Man in the Mirror of the Book*. He was an Argentine novelist and poet who had a worldwide influence.' Another pleasure is a wide variety of music. 'I particularly enjoy Bach, Mozart and Schubert,' he told me, 'and opera and ballet.'

I wanted to know why, in a busy and demanding life as a Bishop, he was prepared to give the time to be involved with the BRF as Chairman of its Council, and why he thinks it is a good organization. This is what he told me:

'From the very earliest days as a Christian, a friend, Richard Hovil, taught me about the vital importance of the Word of God in daily life. And he gave me a verse which I have never forgotten—2 Timothy 2:15.

' "Do your best to present yourself to God as one approved by him, a worker who has no need to be ashamed, rightly explaining the word of truth" (NRSV).

'I am greatly concerned about the lack of daily Bible reading amongst Christians. And I want to do all that I can to encourage it, both in our nation and in other countries. As we draw near to the millennium Christians need to be strengthened and inspired to take forward the cause of God's kingdom and the Good News of Jesus Christ. And BRF is one of the best agencies to do this.'

Shelagh Brown

> '*As we draw near to the millennium Christians need to be strengthened and inspired to take forward the cause of God's kingdom and the Good News of Jesus Christ.*'

Profile of Robert Aldred

Robert Aldred is a teacher at St Edward's School in Oxford. He is also a member of the BRF Council and Executive Committee, and he is Chairman of BRF's Publications Committee.

He and his wife, Alison, have three grown-up children: Sophie, Clare and James.

Robert Aldred has been at St Edward's School for twenty-four years, eleven of them as a House Master of Field House. He was brought up in Reigate, Surrey, and went to school at St Lawrence, Ramsgate. At Durham University he did English, Latin and psychology. 'My first job was teaching in a small school for people with learning difficulties,' he told me, 'in the days before that was usual, and I followed that by teaching at St Lawrence for five years before moving to St Edward's.'

In the sixties Robert was on the team of the Scripture Union Beach Mission at Sheringham (what used to be known as the CSSM), and for four years in the late seventies he was the leader of the team. 'It was great to lead a talented group of young people who were keen to share their faith with others', he

> *'It was great to lead a ... group of young people who were keen to share their faith.'*

said. 'I even took Ali there at the end of our honeymoon and we ended up spending five days there because the team was shortstaffed!'

Alison trained as a nurse, and for some years after they moved to Oxford she worked in the student clinic at University College. It was there that she and Robert met the Chaplain, Bill Sykes, and it was through them that BRF has been able to publish Bill's unique series of *Visions* books. Alison now works as a chiropodist, visiting people in their houses. They live in Weston-on-the-Green, which has been put on the map because that is where the tennis star Tim Henman comes from.

Robert teaches English and Divinity. He also teaches a General Studies Course in Theology and another in Ethics in the Lower and Upper Sixth. In those courses he makes liberal use of Bill Sykes' *Visions* books, which he finds remarkably effective. He helps coach the hockey and also runs the golf at St Edward's. 'I have always had a great interest in sport,' he said, 'and in my more athletic days I was a very keen hockey player and a cricketer. But now I have moved to golf!'

One of his passions is ornithology. 'I birdwatch all the time, even when I'm in the car—much to the annoyance of the family! I've seen red kite flying over the Chilterns—and they are the most marvellous, wonderful creatures. Some pairs were released in the Chilterns and in recent weeks one has been seen flying over Weston. It is my hope that this beautiful bird, which has been persecuted to the point of near extinction, can be re-established in this country. It used to be common over the whole of the British Isles, in the country and in the towns, and it does no harm at all to the human world or to the world of farming. Yet people shoot it and kill it. It feeds on carrion and it's a cleaner-upper of the countryside. It never kills animals itself. But when people put down poison for rabbits it kills the red kite.'

As well as bird watching Robert likes to read. 'But I do it in spurts,' he told me, 'mostly during the holidays. I have just read a wonderful book—*The Railwayman*. It's a marvellous story of forgiveness and a 'must' for everybody. It's about a man who was a prisoner-of-war in Burma and for fifty years sustained a burning hatred for one of his guards. But over those years that same guard had a burning desire for reconciliation—and then, after fifty years, they met.'

'BRF really has a sense of mission—— to serve the churches and to help them and resource them.'

I asked Robert to tell me about his connection with BRF. 'I've found it a fascinating challenge,' he said, 'and it has come at exactly the right time of my life, just after spending eleven years as a housemaster. It is a great opportunity to be involved with something which is outside the school and which is so interesting, and I hope that I can bring something of my experience as a schoolmaster into the work at BRF. What is fascinating, too, is the way in which BRF is developing as an organization. It isn't simply that it is publishing more books now than it ever has in the past, but it really has a sense of mission—to serve the churches and to help them and resource them with the material that it is producing. And the way it is all developing is very, very interesting.'

Shelagh Brown

The Poise of Grace: Life 'in Christ'

Simon Barrington-Ward

It's difficult to recall now that strange period in the sixties when so many young seekers 'dropped out' from their education, or from the 'rat race' into which they felt it led, and set off in search of fulfilment in the mysterious East. So often their hopes came to grief in India or Pakistan, or somewhere on the famous 'trail' to Kabul.

1. The *Dilaram* community

I remember one young man (I'll call him Andrew) for whom this happened. He collapsed in a youth hostel in Delhi. Disappointed by a variety of would-be *gurus* he had taken to drugs and picked up some infection from a dirty needle. So it was that he ended up by being brought into what was called the *Dilaram* community, *dilaram* being the Hindi word for peace.

This was a place where he immediately felt welcomed, cherished and cared for. The rooms were clean, shady, colour-washed in soft tones. They were set in thick walls and cooled by fans. Those who floated round looking after him, European and Asian, men and women, looked like fellow hippies, clad in robes or saris of similar colours to those on the walls.

It soon became clear from the icons around those walls and from the prayers and songs of worship with which they echoed that those who dwelt within them were Christian, in a way which Andrew found attractive and deeply sustaining. A small group of them nursed him through his fever and then through the terrible sensation of being released from the grip of heroin.

Gradually, in this setting, he came to feel strangely comforted and comfortable at every level of his consciousness, physical, emotional and spiritual, as though in some deeply underlying area of himself, he had genuinely 'come home'.

But quite soon there was another awareness dawning on him. Most of those who cared for him were fellow casualties. Even the permanent 'members' were the same. And every one was expected to do the housework and the chores as soon as they could. That, as in all community life, was where the working out of his new peace began. Having been 'given', it now also had to be won. And yet, over all, what you encountered here was always, first and foremost, a culture of acceptance. That sense of mutual forgiveness and forgiven-ness was always primary.

Within its security you could then also find yourself being confronted with your own selfishness, idleness or resentfulness, and coming up against those same tendencies in others, in ways which could be painful. And yet again, even through that sharp encounter, the implicit invitation to admit your own fault was always present. And with this admission, you kept breaking through once more to an even deeper and more far-reaching affirmation of your own value and a release of your gifts in a way which was profoundly healing and helpful.

At the heart of this continuing rhythm of repentance and forgiveness lay shared prayer and worship. Those times of waiting on the presence and love of God together were increasingly central to the common life of *Dilaram* as Andrew experienced it. From such interludes there flowed a wider awareness that the action of grace was setting in motion a continuous breaking and remaking, not only in one's inner self, not only in the life of the community, but in the world at large.

At the heart of this continuing rhythm of repentance and forgiveness lay shared prayer and worship.

It was for Andrew, as for all of those with him, to be part of that breaking and remaking, both by his prayer and in his whole way of living. He was to go out from there committed to this redemptive process in the world around him, in whatever job he found himself called to, in the building of friendships, of future marriage and family perhaps, in social action in politics, in the struggle for justice, for true human community, for the preservation of the planet itself from destruction. For Andrew the quest was no longer so much for a way of being, as for a way of *becoming*.

2. A way of becoming

The source, the theme and the goal of this shared way of life into which Andrew had now entered was 'Christ'. That is to say that from the very beginning the love which was communicated to him as he lay sick in the room to which he had been brought so thankfully, was the love of God, brought home to us all in the person of Jesus Christ.

The teaching of Jesus, his activity, his taking of our burdens upon him in his suffering and death, and the shared, risen life which he opened up to his disciples, through the power of the Spirit he breathed into them: these were the realities constantly informing the whole development of *Dilaram*. They led into a kind of living out of one's baptism together with others, a shared life, a rhythm of constant entering in upon Christ's death and resurrection, of continual rebirth.

'I press on to grasp that for which Christ has already grasped me'

For each and all of us, as for the whole universe, this was a 'way', a journey within which we have already arrived at our goal 'in Christ', as Andrew did when he entered the very door of *Dilaram*, and yet we are also still not there, still, while this world lasts, journeying 'in hope'.

3. The Pauline balance

The realism and the scope of this universal way of becoming are well caught by St Paul, both in Romans chapter 8 and, more personally perhaps, in Philippians chapters 3 and 4. He speaks of being held himself in what appears to be a marvellous balance, poised, like the creation itself, between having arrived and still travelling.

'Not as though I have already attained, or have yet reached perfection, but I press on to grasp that for which Christ has already grasped me' (Philippians 3:12). This is the poise, not of confidence in our own achievement, but of trust, of faith in that love which in Christ has taken hold of us and will freely, with him, in the end give us everything. It is faith which knows 'both how to be abased and how to abound', trusting in that grace, which enables Paul to say, 'I can do all things through Christ which strengthens me' (Philippians 4:12–13).

Nowhere else can there be found quite such a fusion of both failure and hope; commitment to a fully this-worldly life and yet power to reach through and beyond it; a fusion of honesty and vulnerable humility on the one hand and yet of the release of transforming gifts and love on the other. It is here—within the life that flows from trust in the person and cross and resurrection of Christ—that not only Andrew but all of us, and the whole universe of which we are a part, can find a way of becoming, a way that opens up into a new and boundless creation yet to be!

Abusing God's Creation

An extract from Time to Change by Hugh Montefiore

A horrible new strain of the rare Creutszfeldt-Jakob Disease (CJD) in humans has appeared in the last twelve years. It seems to attack younger people, and it takes less time to develop. The sufferer gradually loses his memory, sinks into a coma, and dies. There is no cure.

No one has actually proved as yet a link with Mad Cow Disease (BSE) but it seems probable from experiments with other animals. Most people think that the epidemic of BSE, now ten years old, was caused by a special type of cattle feed, which has also been used as fertiliser on cattle pastures. This was particularly rich in protein because it included the ground up remains of both cattle and sheep.

Some sheep have long been infected by a similar illness called Scrapie (non infectious to humans). Experts believe that the infection has now jumped from one species to another. Scrapie, they think, has become BSE in cattle through the cattle feed and grass they have eaten, and BSE has become CJD in humans through their eating infected beef. These illnesses take a long time to develop, so no one can tell whether we shall suffer a huge epidemic of CJD or there will be only a few more cases. To prevent future infection, thousands of cattle have to be burnt. Until this is done, no one overseas wants to buy our beef. The beef industry is in ruins.

Herbivores have unwittingly been turned into carnivores, even cannibals.

Cattle naturally eat only grass. If this is the origin of CJD, it has been caused by making them consume feed which contains remains of cattle and sheep. Herbivores have unwittingly been turned into carnivores, even cannibals. This shows a gross lack of respect for animals which we human beings have domesticated.

It offends against the natural law of their being. It is a horrible offence for which, it seems, we may be horribly punished.

We have to ask ourselves whether we are treating the natural world today in such a way that we are in danger of bringing upon ourselves not blessings but a curse. God does not strike us directly; but he has so designed the natural world that if we do not respect its proper boundaries, the results rebound upon ourselves. This is one of the spiritual truths to be found in the famous story of Adam and Eve. They were in charge of the Garden of Eden, but they disobeyed the rules of their stewardship. As a result they found that this disobedience rebounded on themselves. 'Cursed is the ground because of you; in toil you shall eat of it all the days of your life' (Genesis 3:17).

It would be wrong to imagine that the curses mentioned in Deuteronomy were all literally fulfilled. But the Old Testament prophets insist that the Jews lost their inheritance in the Holy Land because they had not kept the commandments of God. These commandments were not for the most part concerned with the environment, or with cattle in particular. After all, they were spoken to the children of Israel in a very different situation thousands of years ago.

In those days no one could imagine that they were harming the environment. Much time was taken up in trying to ensure that the environment did not harm them. But the principle holds: if we disobey the natural laws of God, we must expect the judgment of God to come upon us. And this is what is happening today. We are abusing it, and suffering judgment as a result. Some of the correspondences are striking. 'Cursed shall be the increase of your cattle and the young of your flock.' That is precisely what many people today must be thinking about Mad Cow Disease.

If we disobey the natural laws of God, we must expect the judgment of God to come upon us.

'Cursed shall you be in the city' we read. We are prepared to tolerate terrible conditions in our inner cities, and in the favelas and shanty towns of huge conurbations in other countries. The result? Huge increases in crime. For many it has indeed become a curse to live in such places.

'Cursed be the fruit of your body.' Well, not yet; but the mysterious drop in sperm count will affect birth rates if not stemmed. No one is certain what causes it. Some

In John seems old - other boy?
else he mother - brothers)

Look at the boy
face of a chopping of carpentry with Jew?
(where else he of not belize)

Can the father say this weeks
Jesus his ability to think and wants to him

THE WORLD IN WHICH WE LIVE IS
NOT SO ORDINARY; INTENDED BY GOD.

HUMAN WEAKNESS & TRUST — TO WORSHIP SERVING

① JN 1 — JOHN   MORAL THINGS WORK SERVANT — CHRISTIAN
② LK 2:50 PARKVILLE   1020 ?
③ LK 2:11 CHRISTMAS

25) In ... Jerusalem.

A wealthy Pharisee who threw for the poor
farmers who were difficult at the
hands of the powerful landlord.
Jesus who drove churches — compared
with "Jesus Pharisee" who became a
disaster ... better ... Jesus blood".

think it is due to the use of chemicals with particles which mimic elements in the human reproductive system. These chemicals are abroad in the environment, and may threaten not merely human reproduction, but that of animals as well.

As for the threat of diseases, this is all but upon us now, with a new deadly strain of staphylococcus which hospitals find so hard to eradicate and which only one antibiotic can touch. It seems the prodigal and unnecessary use of antibiotics has produced this new type of bacterium. In a rather similar way, patients who did not finish their course of TB treatment have brought about a new airborne strain of this disease which, it is said, is likely to kill thirty million people in the next decade...

In the Bible readings and comments that follow we shall be exploring these and other matters in greater detail. We shall be contrasting our present practices with biblical principles. In the past the Church has been reluctant to concern itself with the environment. Our Christian leaders have not been warning us, and lay Christians have not been in the forefront of the battle.

> *He told them to proclaim God's kingly rule, and to share in it. He calls us to do the same.*

REFLECT AND PRAY

Two thousand years ago Jesus called people to follow him. He calls them still. He gave his first disciples tasks to do. He gives us tasks to do today. He told them to proclaim God's kingly rule, and to share in it. He calls us to do the same. He called people to a change of heart. He calls us too.

Reflect that the risen Christ is always with us. His call to us is as real as it was to Peter and Andrew, and James and John. Then perhaps pray these prayers, or a different prayer of your own.

Jesus, I want to follow you all the days of my life. Show me what you want, and I will do it, with your help.

O God, please show me what I can do to help to restore the environment of your world. Help me to a change of heart, help me to understand, to see clearly and to think clearly. Amen

***

Time to Change is available from your local Christian bookshop or, in case of difficulty, direct from BRF. See the order form on page 159 for details.

CONNECTING WITH GOD
A young person's guide to believing and belonging

If you are responsible for running the Confirmation or Church membership group for young people in your church then *Connecting With God* is for you.

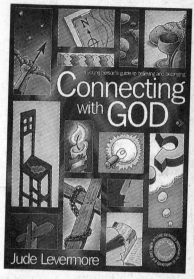

In ten practical and thought-provoking sessions this book aims to get young people thinking about who they are, why the Christian faith is so important, and where they're going in connection with God.

Designed to help young people think for themselves and make up their own minds about life's most important decision, *Connecting With God* looks at the biblical basis of the Christian faith and its implications for young people as individuals within the context of their local church.

Jude Levermore's practical and innovative approach to preparing young people for Confirmation has been warmly welcomed by the young people in her own church. Her tried and tested ideas make this book an ideal resource for all young people wanting to know more about connecting with God, whichever church they belong to.

Jude is a course tutor at Oxford Youth Works, which has gained an excellent reputation in relational youthwork, both in its work with young people and in training others to do it. She is also a Director of Greenbelt Festivals and a Lay Reader in the Diocese of Oxford. She is joint author of *Youthwork and How To Do It*, published by Lynx Communications.

Connecting with God is illustrated by popular cartoonist Simon Smith.

Photocopy permission is included for all worksheet and diary pages which are designed to be built up week by week as a permanent record of the young person's reflections on the course.

Connecting With God takes you through:

 Connecting with Each Other

Connecting with God the Creator

 Connecting with God the Son

Connecting with God the Holy Spirit

 Connecting with God the Father

Connecting with the Bible

 Connecting with Prayer

Connecting with the Church

 Confirming the Connection

Keeping up the Connection

Each session includes:

 PREPARATION AND SESSION AIM
gets you prepared and focused

 FIRST CONNECTIONS
gets your group prepared and focused

 BIBLE CONNECTIONS
explores the session theme through the Bible

 FURTHER CONNECTIONS
expands the teaching

 CONNECTING WITH GOD
explains the teaching

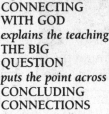 **THE BIG QUESTION**
puts the point across

CONCLUDING CONNECTIONS
draws it together

PERSONAL CONNECTIONS SHEET
(with photocopy permission)
group worksheets and diary pages for individual use by each member of your group

As well as being an excellent foundational introduction to the Christian faith and an ideal preparation for Confirmation, this course also provides you, as a leader in your church, with the springboard for an on-going building of relationships with young people.

All BRF's resources for young people aim to help children in the 11+ age group to explore the Christian faith in the context of their own life experience. We hope that you'll find this exciting course a worthwhile tool in helping your young people to grow towards God.

Connecting with God is available from your local Christian bookshop or, in case of difficulty, direct from BRF. See page 159 for details.

21

Prayer for all Seasons (1)

Joy Tetley

His scream pierced the eerie and untimely darkness. The state's machinery of torture had yet again proved effective. Human gifts of ingenuity and intelligence once more put to the service of inflicting maximum human suffering. Like many before and since, this dying victim was paying the price of standing for truth, where truth proved too threatening.

Like many before and since, this figure crying into the dark was enduring an agony he most certainly did not deserve.

The pain of his execution was compounded by the triumphant taunts of those who wanted rid of him—and had got their way. The words he shouted were difficult to distinguish; distorted, almost throttled by the suffocating pressure on his body. Some, taking perverse pleasure in the event, misheard. But somehow (though this man had been abandoned by his closest friends) true witness emerged—and came to be recorded.

> *This figure crying into the dark was enduring an agony he most certainly did not deserve.*

'My God, my God, why hast thou forsaken me?' Utter desolation. Incomprehension. Determined faithfulness betrayed: not only by human associates but also, it seemed, by God.

Here is prayer at its most basic, raw and elemental. Here, thrown at an absent God, is a question at the heart of human experience: Why? Why? (Not for nothing did Bach emphasize and repeat that word in his *Matthew Passion*). And here is a question that comes straight from the heart of Jesus— right from the core of his being and out of the middle of his desperate situation. The luxury of distanced debate is a million miles away.

Contemplate Jesus, urges the writter of the Epistle to the Hebrews. Look to Jesus. 'See' Jesus. For in so doing, you will see the truth about yourself, the truth about humankind and—most amazingly of all—the truth about God.

It is the claim of Hebrews (and, indeed, of Christians down the ages) that Jesus is the self-expression of God in human form. Looking to Jesus means seeing into the life and character of God. What that implies about God is staggering.

It means that the God who is, by definition, greater than the mysterious immensity of the universe, the God who is source and energy of all creation, this God knows from the inside what it means to be human; knows joy and love and hope and yearning; knows laughter and tears, vitality and weariness; knows fulfilment and frustration, wellbeing and suffering; knows compelling visions and shattered dreams, utter commitment and (from others) radical rejection.

We find someone who can encourage, strengthen and challenge us to the roots, someone who can draw out of us what we hardly realized we had it in us to be.

And somehow, this God even knows what it is like to feel God-forsaken, to feel totally alone. There, truly, is humanity's most profound source of hope. God knows! Hidden in that popular expletive is the Word made flesh. So often we know not what we say. We utter transforming truth, and translate it into empty words.

But truth remains. Truth waits to be discovered. Truth longs to take hold of us for good. For truth is, essentially and eternally, personal and passionate. When we look, openly, to Jesus, such truth is disclosed. We find someone 'like us'; we find someone who can meet us where we are (in every sense of that phrase). We find someone who can go with us, even through hell. We find someone who can encourage, strengthen and challenge us to the roots, someone who can draw out of us what we hardly realized we had it in us to be. We find God.

In Jesus, too, we see humanity as it could and should be. And in Jesus we discover the essence of prayer: a heart-to-heart relationship; from the heart of God to humankind, from the heart of humankind to God—and with complete honesty on both sides.

In exploring such prayer, the Passion of Jesus is a good place to begin, for there the matter is focused most sharply and starkly. So let us look at the night before Christ's death.

'In the same night that he was betrayed,' as the eucharistic prayer so tellingly puts it, Jesus engaged in much prayer. He was facing the greatest crisis of his life. Prayer was his primary and fundamental response. Such had evidently been the case in a variety of situations during his public ministry. It had no doubt also characterized his life in that long hidden period before his baptism in the Jordan. For Jesus, prayer was inseparable from life and work. Prayer was his life-breath. Prayer permeated his being. For prayer was nothing less than living life, with and in God.

In the same night that he was betrayed, 'Jesus took bread, and

For Jesus, prayer was inseparable from life and work. Prayer was his life-breath. Prayer permeated his being. For prayer was nothing less than living life, with and in God.

blessed and broke it, and gave it to the disciples and said, "Take, eat; this is my body". And he took a cup, and when he had given thanks he gave it to them, saying, "Drink of it, all of you; for this is my blood of the covenant, which is poured out for many for the forgiveness of sins"' (Matthew 26:26–28).

They were all sitting at supper, Jesus and the Twelve (and possibly others). It was a scene that must have been repeated many, many times before. Table fellowship was clearly important to Jesus. According to three of the Gospel writers (Matthew, Mark and Luke) this particular supper was a celebratory one, a meal to mark the feast of Passover.

On this occasion, however, Jesus was not just looking back to past bitter oppression from which his people had been delivered. He was looking forward to the bitterness of his own suffering, ultimate expression of the love and forgiveness of God, a new and greater Passover, the offering of a deeper relationship (or covenant) with God.

He gave thanks over bread and wine; a familiar practice, but surely, for Jesus. far more than a mechanical saying of grace. Jesus delighted in the good things of God's creation and saw the presence and messages of God both in *them*, and in the mundane details of everyday life. To borrow George Herbert's phrase, Jesus saw and affirmed 'heaven in ordinarie'.

His teaching is full of it. The lilies of the field, a woman sweeping a room, a parent having problems with children—all these, and many more, are means of discerning the active involvement of God in the world. To Jesus, this was indeed something to rejoice in.

From the whole tenor of his ministry, and from the tantalizing glimpses we have into his prayer life, it seems that Jesus was given to rejoicing and exultation. He exults in the Holy Spirit. He gives thanks to God. He is full of vitality and *joie-de-vivre*. Tragically, it is the blinkered vision and fearful hardness of heart of the formal religious establishment that, in the end, hammers the joy out of him.

Even so, it burst out again 'with a vengeance' on Easter morning. Whatever the provocation, God and joy will not be finally separated. To the ages of ages, they belong together.

Bread and wine. Staple of life, and that which makes the heart glad. Reason enough to give thanks. But now, after this momentous supper, there is more. Now bread and wine become 'outward and visible signs' of the redeeming self-giving of God, that God from whom we derive both life and gladness.

As we eat and drink in faith, the reality to which the signs point nourishes our being. Our joy and pain are united with the pain and joy of God.

> *Jesus delighted in the good things of God's creation and saw the presence and messages of God both in them, and in the mundane details of everyday life.*

Holiday Reading

Shelagh Brown

When he goes on holidays a vicar I know always takes lots of books with him to read. They fall into two clearly defined categories: secular books (detective stories and novels) and theological books. And he invariably reads the detective stories and novels first, and brings back the theological books almost invariably unopened. I used to do just the same—but as I have got a bit older I have become a bit wiser. Now I take just *one* religious book and really feed on it—so long as I'm feeling hungry for it.

For me that works—and I remember one year sitting on the beach at St Ives in Cornwall reading an old classic: *The Spirit of God* by Dr Campbell Morgan. I was exhilarated by it—and I could see the sheer efficiency and glory of God's plan of salvation (the Holy Spirit of God lives *in* us) far more clearly and understand it far more deeply. John Polkinghorne's *Science and the Providence of God* had the same exhilarating and enlarging effect when I was on my ordination retreat before being priested.

> *One of the most important things I learned ... was the truth that 'We can't do everything!'*

Recently I went on a course on managing priorities and meeting deadlines and one of the most important things I learned from it was the truth that 'We can't do everything!' I don't like having to believe it (and I'm having to work quite hard on doing so) because I feel that if only I worked harder and was more organized then I *would* be able to do everything. Or at least, everything I want to do. And that's true of reading as well as other things. It's all right to put everything down on our 'To Read List'—and make sure we have a selection of subjects. Some spiritual and theological books (not every one reviewed in *Theology* or *The Church of England Newspaper* or *Renewal*), some of the latest popular paperbacks, and a classic or two. But then we need to pull out the priorities and make a realistic and sensible choice: for most of us just *one* spiritual or theological book—and the rest of them for relaxation. That's what holidays are for, and we need them.

Holidays come from holy days, so *some* spiritual reading is good and necessary for our re-creation and refreshing, and our spirits need feeding and exercising just as our bodies do. St Ignatius knew what he was doing when he created The Spiritual Exercises, and in the hundreds of years since he wrote about them and explained how to use them thousands of people have discovered their enormous value.

We need to make a realistic choice... just one spiritual or theological book—and the rest of them for relaxation.

This article is about holiday reading in general, not about BRF books in particular. You may well have one particular book in mind for your spiritual reading. If not, then I offer you a suggestion. One of Bill Sykes' *Visions* books would give you some rich and varied food for thought and meditation. Choose just one subject a day—and enjoy it.

The *Visions* series is available from your local Christian bookshop or, in case of difficulty, direct from BRF. See order form on page 159 for details.

The unregretfulness of God

John Fenton

It must, of course, be true that there is a vast difference between God as he is, and our ideas about him. If it were not so, he would not be God. We can only take in as much as we have the capacity for understanding, and, in the case of God, that must be less than the whole truth.

Nevertheless, it does not follow from this that it does not matter what we say about God, or what we think about him. There are still mistakes that can be made, or so those who believe in God will always maintain. He is not cruel or uncaring; he has no competitors; it is not true that he does not exist. One idea about God that seems to have gained popularity recently is that he is disappointed, heartbroken, in despair; that he regrets ever having made the world, and that he wishes he had never permitted the existence of human beings.

There is some support in scrip-

> *One idea about God that seems to have gained popularity recently is that he is disappointed, heart-broken, in despair.*

ture for thinking about God in this way. For example, in the introduction to the story of the flood:

'When the Lord saw how great was the wickedness of human beings on earth, and how their every thought and inclination were always wicked, he bitterly regretted that he had made mankind on earth.' (Genesis 6:5,6)

Though it should be noticed that the story ends with God's promise that he will never again put the earth under a curse because of mankind (8:21); the rainbow is the sign of this covenant (9:12–14). Another example of divine regretfulness in scripture is the appointment of Saul as king (1 Samuel 15:11, 35). In contrast with this is a group of passages in which it is said that God does not change his mind; for example, there is Balaam's question:

'God is not a mortal that he should lie, not a man that he should change his mind. Would he speak, and not make it good? What he proclaims, will he not fulfil?' (Numbers 23:19)

A notable instance of a biblical writer affirming the unregretfulness of God comes in Paul's letter to the Romans; the translation of it in the Revised English Bible is: 'The gracious gifts of God and his calling are irrevocable' (Romans 11:29).

More literally, with the word to be emphasized at the beginning of the sentence, it could be reordered:

'Not to be regretted are the free gifts and the calling of God'—meaning, God does not regret what he has done in giving his gifts to Israel and in calling them his people. (The only other place in the New Testament where the word here translated 'not to be regretted'

God is not to be thought of as one who has failed; he does not back losers; he is not incompetent; he has wisdom and knowledge incomparable

occurs is in 2 Corinthians 7:10, where Paul says that the Corinthians' previous pain caused by his letter to them will not be regretted, by him or by them.)

The argument in Romans 9 and 11 is that though the unbelief of the majority of Jews causes Paul great grief and unceasing sorrow in his heart (9:2), he still looks forward to the time when God's purpose will be worked out fully, in mercy to all mankind (11:2). God is not to be thought of as one who has failed; he does not back losers; he is not incompetent; he has wisdom and knowledge incomparable (11:33–36).

To think otherwise would be to make God in our image and to attribute to him the limitations under which we live. It is frequently a consequence of our ignorance that we act in ways that lead us to disappointment and regret: we are taken in by people, or we are blind to their faults, or we fail to take account of circumstances. None of this can apply to God. He knows what he is doing and he can foresee the consequences of it—so Paul believed; and it is hard to think otherwise of God. Even the consequences of human freedom need not be thought the cause of God's failure, as though it took him by surprise. 'Would he speak, and not make it good?', as Balaam asked; must we not think of him as foreseeing and containing within his good purpose everything that would or could happen?

How did Paul come to be able to state so clearly the unregretfulness of God? Possibly it was through reflecting on the crucifixion and resurrection of Jesus. On a purely human view, the death of Jesus looked like the failure of a mission: he had persuaded no one to stand by him, according to Mark; his followers had run away, betrayed him and dis-

We have become so used to responding to appeals for our sympathy, that we even suppose that we should be sorry for God.

owned him. But this was not the whole of the matter. Paul had at one time thought it was, but now he sees that it was not. 'The folly of God is wiser than human wisdom, and the weakness of God stronger than human strength' (1 Corinthians 1:25). What happened was meant to happen.

Regret, sense of failure, disappointment, unhappiness, should not be attributed to God, but wisdom, skill, knowledge, complete and inevitable eventual success; and above all, joy. We have become so used to responding to appeals for our sympathy, that we even suppose that we should be sorry for God. This is no way to think of the one who is the beginning and the end of all things, blessed for ever; nor is it any way to help people to believe in him. No one wants yet another person to be sorry for.

John Fenton *is the author of* The Matthew Passion, *and of* Galatians *in the* People's Bible Commentary *Series. Both are published by BRF and are available from your local Christian bookshop or, in case of difficulty, direct from BRF. For details, see order form, page 159.*

Colossians 1:3–8 (NRSV)

The seed of love

In our prayers for you we always thank God, the Father of our Lord Jesus Christ, for we have heard of your faith in Christ Jesus and of the love that you have for all the saints, because of the hope laid up for you in heaven. You have heard of this hope before in the word of the truth, the gospel that has come to you. Just as it is bearing fruit and growing in the whole world, so it has been bearing fruit among yourselves from the day you heard it and truly comprehended the grace of God. This you learned from Epaphras, our beloved fellow servant. He is a faithful minister of Christ on your behalf, and he has made known to us your love in the Spirit.

In this letter the apostle Paul makes the most awesome statements about the nature of Jesus Christ. As we read his words we shall find them all the more astonishing if we keep remembering that Paul had been the strictest of Jews. For them and for him there was one Creator God—the Lord—and to worship a creature or to bow down before the likeness of any creature was idolatry. Now Paul still worshipped and adored the one Creator God—but his meeting with Christ on the road to Damascus had transformed his understanding. Now he was 'an apostle of Christ Jesus by the will of God' and he worshipped his Lord—Jesus Christ.

The Colossian Christians were mostly Gentiles. They hadn't heard the Good News from Paul, but probably from Epaphras—and even if he, Epaphras, hadn't actually founded the church, he was ministering to it now. He had told Paul (who had never even seen these Christians) of their 'love in the Spirit', and Paul's immediate response was to start praying for them and to write to them.

The seed of the gospel had taken root in them and was growing into a great tree laden with delicious and attractive fruit—qualities which are deeply satisfying to have in ourselves and to meet in someone else. 'The fruit of the Spirit is love, joy, peace, patience, kindness, generosity, faithfulness, gentleness, and self-control' (Galatians 5:22–23).

Reflect

How well is the tree of life and the gospel growing and bearing fruit in my life—in my church—and in the places where I live and work?

SB

Colossians 1:9–14 (NRSV)

An apostle's prayer

For this reason, since the day we heard it, we have not ceased praying for you and asking that you may be filled with the knowledge of God's will in all spiritual wisdom and understanding, so that you may lead lives worthy of the Lord, fully pleasing to him, as you bear fruit in every good work and as you grow in the knowledge of God. May you be made strong with all the strength that comes from his glorious power, and may you be prepared to endure everything with patience, while joyfully giving thanks to the Father, who has enabled you to share in the inheritance of the saints in the light. He has rescued us from the power of darkness and transferred us into the kingdom of his beloved Son, in whom we have redemption, the forgiveness of sins.

Paul's prayer for those Colossian Christians is a very big prayer, asking for great things for them. But then he knows how great God is—and how great his power is and how great his plans and purposes are for all his people and for all the world. Years ago J.B. Phillips wrote a book called *Your God Is Too Small*. But Paul's God wasn't too small. He was unimaginably great and glorious—and sometimes when Paul is writing about him he feels overwhelmed with his glory and bursts into praise. Incidentally, J.B. Phillips used to be Vicar of St Matthew's, Redhill, where Canon Mannering, the founder of BRF, had been Vicar. J.B. Phillips translated the New Testament into modern English because he knew how vital it was for every Christian to read and understand the written word of God.

Paul wasn't either a liar or a muddled thinker. Anything but. So if he prayed that vast prayer for them then he knew it could happen. Will you go back and read it again now?

All those glorious possibilities were the will of God for those early Christians and they are also the will of God for each one of us. The 'glorious power' that brings the possibilities into existence is the same power which created the world and raised Christ from the dead. More of that tomorrow. For today, pray the passage for yourself and for your church.

A way to pray

First, pray the passage aloud and say 'I' instead of 'you'. Then pray it again and say 'we' instead of 'you'.

SJ

Colossians 1:15–17 (NRSV)

Christ the creator

2,000 years ago a baby was born in a stable in Bethlehem. When he grew up he spent three years preaching and teaching, making disciples and making sick people well again. Then he was nailed to a cross and put to death on a hill outside Jerusalem. But on the third day after he died he appeared to some of his followers—who then went all over the known world preaching 'Jesus and resurrection'. A Jew called Paul persecuted them and was responsible for putting some of them to death. But then the man who had died but was alive again appeared to Paul. Some years later this is what Paul wrote about him:

He is the image of the invisible God, the firstborn of all creation; for in him all things in heaven and on earth were created, things visible and invisible, whether thrones or dominions or rulers or powers—all things have been created through him and for him. He himself is before all things, and in him all things hold together.

That is an impossible thing to say about a human being. But this human being was also the divine being—God incarnate. 'Truly God and truly man.' God in human form. We often think about the human Jesus. But to be aware of the true greatness of the glory of Christ we have to contemplate the God-dimension of his nature—'for in him all things in heaven and earth were created...'

Part of Paul's purpose in writing to the Colossians was to deal with the gnostic heresy, which claimed amongst other things that the Creator-God had distanced himself from his creation, and was separated from it by a series of emanations. Jesus was just one of these, they said—and he was spirit. He appeared in a body so as to reveal God, but he couldn't really be flesh and blood because matter was evil. Paul says that is utterly wrong. What he wrote was a definitive counter-claim to gnostic teaching—and it also has something to say to us in our scientific age.

In those days they didn't realize the vastness of the universe with all its billions of stars. But they knew it was far bigger than they were and that there were so many stars in the heavens that no one could ever count them. And the New Testament says that the power which brought all that into being and holds it all in existence is the power of Christ.

A contemplation

Read Paul's words again. Then be silent and let the awesomeness of them sink into you.

SB

John 16:25–27 (NEB)

Ask in my name...

'Till now I have been using figures of speech; a time is coming when I shall no longer use figures, but tell you of the Father in plain words. When that day comes you will make your request in my name, and I do not say that I shall pray to the Father for you, for the Father loves you himself, because you have loved me and believed that I came from God.'

Jesus is making an astonishing promise to the disciples (and to us)— but it isn't an unconditional promise. We can pray direct to the Father and make our requests known to him. But we have to ask in the name of Jesus.

That doesn't mean asking for whatever it is we want and then just tacking on the name at the end. 'Father, please may I pass my exam... please can our team win the match... please may John/Mary fall in love with me. For Jesus' sake...'

That isn't how prayer works. To make a request 'in my name' is to ask for something which is in line with the will of God as Jesus has made it known to us. 'Your will be done' is the prayer that gathers up all prayers into itself. But to look at Jesus and ask what the will of God might be in a particular situation is to take the risk of getting a tough answer. 'My Father, if it is possible, let this cup pass from me; yet not what I want but what you want.' What the Father wanted for the Son was for him to die on the cross and suffer for the sin of the world.

Years ago I used to be afraid that if I really prayed 'Your will be done', God would send me to the other side of the world to do it—and I didn't want to go and I didn't feel that as an only child of elderly and ailing parents that I ought to go. But I was forgetting about the love of God—for them and for me.

Some of the prayers that Paul starts his letters with are perfect models of the things we should be asking for. Look back for a moment at the prayer on Friday 2 May. Then spend some time reflecting on what your life might be like if you prayed it and God gave you your request.

SB

Colossians 1:18–20 (NRSV)

Firstborn

He is the head of the body, the church; he is the beginning, the firstborn from the dead, so that he might come to have first place in everything. For in him all the fullness of God was pleased to dwell, and through him God was pleased to reconcile to himself all things, whether on earth or in heaven, by making peace through the blood of his cross.

Jesus Christ is 'the firstborn of creation' and 'the firstborn from the dead', but the meaning of firstborn in those phrases is different. In English 'the firstborn of creation' (in yesterday's reading) sounds as if God the creator was there at the beginning and that the first thing he did was to create Jesus. But William Barclay says that 'in Hebrew and Greek thought, firstborn (*protokos*) has only very indirectly a time significance at all. Firstborn is very commonly a title of honour...'. For the Jews, Psalm 89:27 was a promise about the Messiah: 'I will make him my firstborn, higher than the kings of the earth'; and here it is 'not used in a time sense at all, but in the sense of special honour'.

When we get to the glory of heaven we shall be worshipping in the Spirit before the throne of God and of the Lamb—the firstborn of creation and the one through whom and for whom all things were created.

The words 'the firstborn from the dead' are about the resurrection of Jesus Christ from the dead—'the first-born within a large family' (Romans 8:29). Jesus first, then us. But not only us. It is not only human creatures who are going to be reconciled to God through Jesus Christ. God has made other creatures too—lions and whales and blackbirds, and insects and trees and plants. The Old Testament and the New tell of a redemption for all those things as well as for us:

To think about

I consider that the sufferings of this present time are not worth comparing with the glory about to be revealed to us. For the creation waits with eager longing for the revealing of the children of God; for the creation was subjected to futility, not of its own will but by the will of the one who subjected it, in hope that the creation itself will be set free from its bondage to decay and will obtain the freedom of the glory of the children of God.

Romans 8:18–21

SB

Colossians 1:21–23 (NRSV)

Reconciliation

And you who were once estranged and hostile in mind, doing evil deeds, he has now reconciled in his fleshly body through death, so as to present you holy and blameless and irreproachable before him—provided that you continue securely established and steadfast in the faith, without shifting from the hope promised by the gospel that you heard, which has been proclaimed to every creature under heaven. I, Paul, became a servant of this gospel.

We don't have to understand how 'God was in Christ reconciling the world to himself' (2 Corinthians 5:19). All we have to do is to accept that it happened and believe in the almost incredible truth of it. We can ask for forgiveness—and it will be given to us. But we can't have it apart from God-in-Christ, who desires to give us himself as well as his forgiveness. Forgiveness isn't an abstract thing. It is about reconciliation between persons. My Christian life began when my sins were forgiven and I was reconciled to God—and the same goes for you. But that's the beginning—not the end.

The start of our Christian life (whenever it took place—and we may not know) has to do with our initial forgiveness. Our sins are wiped out and removed and we receive the Spirit of Christ into our hearts. Justification is the technical term for that—and it has been defined as 'Just as if I'd never sinned'. Christ gives us forgiveness and gives us himself. We have a new start and a new life in Christ—but the person we were before that happened hasn't been blotted out of existence. We still have the same body and the same brain, with the same past and the same memories. The difference is that the Holy Spirit of Christ is within us. If we follow his leading then we shall be able to live a holy life. The technical term for that process is sanctification—and it is the work of the Holy Spirit in us, making us like Christ.

Reflect

Spend some time reflecting on what Paul says that Christ will do one day, now that he has reconciled us to God: present us holy and blameless and irreproachable before him. Reflect on that hope that has been promised to us in the gospel. Pray that we shall be established in the faith and continue 'steadfast in the faith'.

SB

Colossians 1:24–26 (NRSV)

Suffering for your sake and his

I am now rejoicing in my sufferings for your sake, and in my flesh I am completing what is lacking in Christ's afflictions for the sake of his body, that is, the church. I became its servant according to God's commission that was given to me for you, to make the word of God fully known, the mystery that has been hidden throughout the ages and generations but has now been revealed to his saints.

Paul really did have a total turnaround on the road to Damascus when the risen Christ met him there. Then on his way to persecute the Christians and make them suffer, now he was suffering for their sake and and for the sake of his ministry to them. The Jew who had persecuted the Christians and despised the Gentiles had been commissioned to preach the word of God to the Gentiles so that they became Christians.

We shall look on Friday at 'the mystery that has been hidden through the ages and generations'. Today we are reflecting on the fact that it has been revealed to us—and that the revelation is given through the word of God. Whether it is preached or read it is through the word that we get to know the good news of the love of God for 'every creature under heaven'. The word is a seed that takes root in our hearts and grows. Like a baby—starting very small within its mother's womb. Like a tiny acorn—growing into a great oak tree. Life and growth both happen through the word.

Paul's commission from God was to 'make the word of God fully known'. In the process of doing this he would suffer. When Ananias was sent to Paul to lay hands on him after his Damascus road experience (and suggesting to the Lord he saw in his vision that it might be a bit unwise to go) he was told that 'I myself will show him how much he must suffer for the sake of my name'(Acts 9:16). The suffering of Christ was a 'complete, perfect and sufficient sacrifice for the sins of the whole world.' But there is a cost to preaching the gospel and building up the body of Christ. That is what Paul and all of us have to complete in the sufferings of Christ for the people that he loves.

Reflect

How are we completing what is lacking in the sufferings of Christ in our generation?

SB

Acts 1:1–9 (part) (GNB)

Ascension Day

Dear Theophilus: In my first book I wrote about all the things that Jesus did and taught from the time he began his work until the day he was taken up to heaven. Before he was taken up, he gave instructions by the power of the Holy Spirit to the men he had chosen as his apostles. For forty days after his death he appeared to them many times in ways that proved beyond doubt that he was alive. They saw him, and he talked with them about the Kingdom of God... they asked him, 'Lord, will you at this time give the Kingdom back to Israel?' Jesus said to them, 'The times and occasions are set by my Father's own authority, and it is not for you to know when they will be. But when the Holy Spirit comes upon you, you will be filled with power, and you will be witnesses for me in Jerusalem, in all Judaea and Samaria, and to the ends of the earth'. After saying this, he was taken up to heaven as they watched him, and a cloud hid him from their sight.

In the days just before he died Jesus was telling his disciples what lay ahead. 'A little while, and you will no longer see me,' he said, 'and again a little while, and you will see me' (John 16:16). And that is what happened. For a little while they didn't see him, as he lay dead in the darkness of the tomb. Then he was raised from the dead and they did see him. But after the resurrection appearances there is a final disappearance, and this is what we are celebrating on Ascension Day. Yet they might not have felt like celebrating, because the Jesus they could see was taken away from them.

Now they had to wait for something to happen. It would be even better than having the human Jesus with them and even better than the appearances of the risen Jesus. They didn't know that then. But perhaps they were sure enough of him now to trust him as they waited—and even to praise him—knowing that God could change sorrow into joy and death into eternal life. Perhaps when we are finding life difficult and feeling sad—and wondering and waiting to know what lies ahead—the Ascension and the waiting that followed it can help us to lift up our hearts and to praise God.

SB

Colossians 1:27—2:3 (NRSV)

Christ in you

To them God chose to make known how great among the Gentiles are the riches of the glory of this mystery, which is Christ in you, the hope of glory. It is he whom we proclaim, warning everyone and teaching everyone in all wisdom, so that we may present everyone mature in Christ. For this I toil and struggle with all the energy that he powerfully inspires within me. For I want you to know how much I am struggling for you, and for those in Laodicea, and for all who have not seen me face to face. I want their hearts to be encouraged and united in love, so that they may have all the riches of assured understanding and have the knowledge of God's mystery, that is, Christ himself, in whom are hidden all the treasures of wisdom and knowledge.

The 'them' to whom God chose to make the mystery known were the saints—and the saints are all the people of God, not just the special ones. And the chosen people of God were now Gentiles as well as Jews.

The glory and the wonder of this mystery is 'Christ in you, the hope of glory'—and it is an awesome truth. We were looking a few days ago at the nature of the Christ we worship—the one through whom and for whom all things were created. The one who made our world with all its marvellous variety of living things, and the stars which are millions of light years away in the furthest galaxies of the universe, some of them (they tell us) moving out into space faster than the speed of light.

The Christ who holds all things in existence and who made all things is the 'Christ in us, the hope of glory'. Paul struggled to 'present everyone mature in Christ'—and that is what God wants for each one of us. It is what every pastor wants for a congregation and it is what we should want for ourselves. Not to be feeble, undeveloped Christians, like weedy plants that have never grown and never had enough light or food. But full grown and fruitful—to the glory of God.

Reflect

Spend some time reflecting on the truth of 'Christ in you, the hope of glory'—and on the awesomeness of his nature. Then spend some time in silence, worshipping.

SB

The fulness of Christ

As you therefore have received Christ Jesus the Lord, continue to live your lives in him, rooted and built up in him and established in the faith, just as you were taught, abounding in thanksgiving. See to it that no one takes you captive through philosophy and empty deceit, according to human tradition, according to the elemental spirits of the universe, and not according to Christ. For in him the whole fulness of deity dwells bodily, and you have come to fullness in him, who is the head of every ruler and authority. In him also you were circumcised with a spiritual circumcision, by putting off the body of the flesh in the circumcision of Christ; when you were buried with him in baptism, you were also raised with him through faith in the power of God, who raised him from the dead.

We are to live our Christian lives in the same way that we began them—in the Spirit, and by faith not works. We are rooted in Christ—rooted and grounded in love—and it is in love and through love that we grow, doing everything out of love for him—or, often, *not* doing it out of love for him. God wants us to grow up into Christian maturity, and giving thanks is one of the ways to grow. Gerard W. Hughes, the writer on spirituality (and author of *Oh God, Why?* published by BRF) suggests that every night when we go to bed we review our day and thank God for particular things that have happened. Oddly, giving thanks can help in the sorrow of bereavement. 'Thank you that I knew him', we can say. 'Thank you for that particular thing I remember about him... about her. As we remember and give thanks, the dark-ness of our sorrow is somehow light-ened. The sorrow doesn't go away, but in some way it is changed.

Paul's words about the whole full-ness of deity dwelling in Christ flatly contradict the belief of the Gnostics. The deity is not distanced from us. St Augustine wrote that 'He is closer to me than my breathing', and Paul would have agreed. The one who is closer to us than our breathing is the one in whom all the fullness of deity dwells—and that one dwells in us.

A way to pray

'*Rejoice always, pray without ceasing, give thanks in all circumstances; for this is the will of God in Christ Jesus for you.*

1 Thessalonians 5: 16–18

SB

Ephesians 1:15–20 (TEV)

The power of God in us

Ever since I heard of your faith in the Lord Jesus and your love for all God's people, I have not stopped giving thanks to God for you. I remember you in my prayers and ask the God of our Lord Jesus Christ, the glorious Father, to give you the Spirit, who will make you wise and reveal God to you, so that you will know him. I ask that your minds may be opened to see his light, so that you will know what is the hope to which he has called you, how rich are the wonderful blessings he promises his people, and how very great is his power at work in us who believe. The power working in us is the same as the mighty strength which he used when he raised Christ from death and seated him at his right side in the heavenly world.

This is a wonderful prayer to come right in the middle of our Bible notes on Colossians because it puts together so many of the things that Paul says in that letter. It points us to the glory of God—Father, Son and Spirit. It shows us what a rich relationship we can have with God, and what enormous power and vast resources are there for us in Christ.

When God gives us the Spirit he is giving us himself, day after day after day. It's like a marriage. At the start of it the husband and wife commit themselves to one another and give themselves to one another. Then they go on doing that throughout their lives. 'All that I am I give to you, and all that I have I share with you, within the love of God' it says in the marriage service, and the giving and the sharing go on and on and on and get richer and richer.

'How rich are the wonderful blessings he promises his people', the prayer continues—and we can find out how rich they are by searching them out in the scriptures and asking God to keep every one of the promises he has made.

'How very great is his power at work in us who believe'—and when we realize what he has used that power to do we are stunned. He made the worlds and he raised the dead.

Will you pray the prayer now? For yourself, for the Christians in your church and in the wider church, and for us at BRF?

SB

Colossians 2:13–19 (NRSV)

Wiped out

And when you were dead in trespasses and the uncircumcision of your flesh, God made you alive together with him, when he forgave us all our trespasses, erasing the record that stood against us with its legal demands. He set this aside, nailing it to the cross. He disarmed the rulers and authorities and made a public example of them, triumphing over them in it. Therefore do not let anyone condemn you in matters of food and drink or of observing festivals, new moons, or sabbaths. These are only a shadow of what is to come, but the substance belongs to Christ. Do not let anyone disqualify you, insisting on self-abasement and worship of angels, dwelling on visions, puffed up without cause by a human way of thinking, and not holding fast to the head, from whom the whole body, nourished and held together by its ligaments and sinews, grows with a growth that is from God.

The people who were misleading the Colossians were obviously adding a great list of requirements to the one thing that was necessary for salvation—faith in Christ. So Paul reminds the Christians in this young church of the transformation the gospel had brought about for them. They had been dead in their sins, but now through faith God had made them alive in Christ. Each one of them (and each one of us) has a great list of sins we have done wrong. Or rather, God has the lists. The God who loves us and knows all about us has a record of everything that we have done—or have failed to do.

In the ancient world they wrote on papyrus or vellum—and because that was expensive, and because their ink had no acid in it, a scribe could take a sponge and wipe out all the writing. And Paul says that is just what God has done with the record of our sins: wiped them out as if they had never been. So the Colossians musn't let anyone take that truth away from them nor insist on their doing other things. The death of Christ on the cross is all that is ever needed for sins to be forgiven. Once we have asked God to forgive us he does so at once. Then we live in Christ and Christ lives in us—and all we have to do is to grow up as beloved children into Christian maturity.

A way to pray

Reflect on the glory of forgiveness and thank God for wiping out your sins.

SB

Colossians 2:20—3:4 (NRSV)

With Christ

If with Christ you died to the elemental spirits of the universe, why do you live as if you still belonged to the world? Why do you submit to regulations, 'Do not handle, Do not taste, Do not touch'? ... These have indeed an appearance of wisdom in promoting self-imposed piety, humility, and severe treatment of the body, but they are of no value in checking self-indulgence. So if you have been raised with Christ, seek the things that are above, where Christ is, seated at the right hand of God. Set your minds on things that are above, not on things that are on earth, for you have died, and your life is hidden with Christ in God. When Christ who is your life is revealed, then you also will be revealed with him in glory.

In some ways it is easier to have a set of regulations laid out and written down. Then we can tick them off our list and feel that we have done what we should have done. But the Christian life is both tougher and simpler than that because it is our total life. Our personal life and our public life—all our relationships and all our actions—are all part of the person we are. Sometimes when the media reveal that a public figure has been having an extra-marital affair people will say that someone's private life has nothing to do with their public life. But that isn't true. What happens in one area of our life affects all the others, and if we belong to Christ then the whole of us belongs to him.

To set our mind 'on things that are above' is to be aware all the time that Christ is at the right hand of God—the place which symbolizes the power of God. Our life is in his life, and his life is in ours—'Christ in us, the hope of glory'. Immanent as well as transcendent. Present in all things as well as above all things.

Reflection

Reflect on the truth that you have died with Christ—and that you have been raised up with Christ. Think about your life hidden in Christ, seated at the right hand of God—mediator of the power of God. Reflect on that Christ living in you as you live your life in the world that God loves. He is the light of the world, and so are we.

SB

Colossians 3:5–11 (NRSV)

Tough instructions

Put to death, therefore, whatever in you is earthly: fornication, impurity, passion, evil desire, and greed (which is idolatry). On account of these the wrath of God is coming on those who are disobedient. These are the ways you also once followed, when you were living that life. But now you must get rid of all such things—anger, wrath, malice, slander, and abusive language from your mouth. Do not lie to one another, seeing that you have stripped off the old self with its practices and have clothed yourselves with the new self, which is being renewed in knowledge according to the image of its creator. In that renewal there is no longer Greek and Jew, circumcised and uncircumcised, barbarian, Scythian, slave and free; but Christ is all and in all!

Today we shall look at the things in our lives that we have to put to death and the clothes that we have to take off. Tomorrow we shall look at the new clothes God wants us to wear and at the new life that we live in Christ.

Today's list is a tough one—and some people who say they are Christians don't seem to think they have to pay much attention to it. Fornication is fashionable. It happens all the time in our day (and so does adultery) either in practice or in fantasy. God created sex, and we only have to read the Song of Songs to get our understanding of God's attitude to sex put right. But God's only alternative to married love is chastity. All the sins on Paul's list are a failure in Christian loving, and all of them hurt and damage other people. Only yesterday someone was so abusive on the telephone to someone in our office that when the phone call ended she began to weep.

Paul sets out all the sins that we have to get rid of and then tells us to put on the clothes of the new self. Day by day God renews that new self in us so that we are transformed—transformed by the renewing of our minds (Romans 12:2), which means that we reprogramme them and correct their false knowledge. The source of true knowledge is the word of God.

A way to pray

Spend some time thinking about the end result of each of the sins on Paul's list—and reflect on the way each one affects the person at the receiving end of them.

SB

Colossians 3:12–21 (NRSV)

Put on love

As God's chosen ones, holy and beloved, clothe yourselves with compassion, kindness, humility, meekness, and patience. Bear with one another and, if anyone has a complaint against another, forgive each other; just as the Lord has forgiven you, so you also must forgive. Above all, clothe yourselves with love, which binds everything together in perfect harmony. And let the peace of Christ rule in your hearts, to which indeed you were called in the one body. And be thankful. Let the word of Christ dwell in you richly; teach and admonish one another in all wisdom; and with gratitude in your hearts sing psalms, hymns, and spiritual songs to God. And whatever you do, in word or deed, do everything in the name of the Lord Jesus, giving thanks to God the Father through him.

They are beautiful clothes that God wants us to wear. The garment that everyone will see first is love, because we put that on top of all the other qualities. We know the enormous difference between being with someone who loves us and someone who doesn't. The water lilies in my small pond only open out their petals when the sun is shining—and we only blossom fully as human beings when the light of love is shining on us.

The outside garment of love has other qualities within it and underneath it. If you have time, spend a few moments reading the first sentence of today's passage and reflecting on the meaning of the qualities Paul tells us to put on.

He also tells us to admonish one another—and to admonish means to exhort a person to do what he (or she) should do; to give advice; to warn about something; to inform, and to remind about something. The person who is being admonished doesn't always welcome it, but it is an important part of Christian living and growing. The details of what we are to admonish someone about are all there in the word of Christ. But we are never to take off that outer garment of love—so the person being admonished knows how much they are loved. If we have a problem with the loving then we had better leave the admonishing to someone else.

A way to pray

Do the same exercise as yesterday—but reflect on the qualities that we are to put on after we have taken the others off.

SB

Colossians 3:18–23 (NRSV)

Treat each one like Jesus

Wives, be subject to your husbands, as is fitting in the Lord. Husbands, love your wives and never treat them harshly. Children, obey your parents in everything, for this is your acceptable duty in the Lord. Fathers, do not provoke your children, or they may lose heart. Slaves, obey your earthly masters in everything, not only while being watched and in order to please them, but wholeheartedly, fearing the Lord. Whatever your task, put yourselves into it, as done for the Lord and not for your masters.

Two thousand years ago a wife was her husband's possession. She was a 'thing' which could (but shouldn't) be coveted, along with a neighbour's house, ox, ass or any other thing that was his. Christianity started to change all that, but not overnight. In Christ all the old divisions between groups of people had been broken down—now there was 'neither Jew nor Greek, slave nor free, male nor female'. Individuals didn't stop being Greeks or slaves or women, but they were all 'in Christ' and all Christians. That gave them a sense of value and status which they had never had before, and each one of them was a son or a daughter of the living God..

That was heady stuff. And if it went to a woman's head she might bring dishonour to the Christian faith through her newfound freedom. So she was to be 'subject' to her husband. But Ephesians 5:21 tells every member of the Christian family to 'Be be subject one to another out of reverence for Christ' before it goes on to be specific about wives and husbands. Husbands are to love their wives 'as they do their own bodies' (5:28), which is a very protective and cherishing love. It was a transformation of the marriage relationship. The same goes for children. All our relationships are in Christ so we are to love our children with the same love and treat them in the same way that God the Father loves and treats us.

It has taken far too long for Christians to realize that slavery is wrong. But if a slave could serve his or her owner as if they were serving Christ it would have transformed the slave's attitude—and perhaps had a profound effect on the slave owner.

Think

Do I treat everyone as if they were Jesus?

SB

Colossians 4:2-6, 18 (NRSV)

A door for the word

Devote yourselves to prayer, keeping alert in it with thanksgiving. At the same time pray for us as well that God will open to us a door for the word, that we may declare the mystery of Christ, for which I am in prison, so that I may reveal it clearly, as I should. Conduct yourselves wisely towards outsiders, making the most of the time. Let your speech always be gracious, seasoned with salt, so that you may know how you ought to answer everyone... ' I, Paul, write this greeting with my own hand. Remember my chains. Grace be with you.

Paul began this letter by telling the Colossian Christians that he was praying for them. He finishes it by telling them to pray. To devote themselves to prayer and to pray for him. He was in a Roman prison, probably handcuffed to a member of the praetorian guard. 'It has become known throughout the whole imperial guard and to everyone else that my imprisonment is for Christ' Paul wrote to the Philippians (1:13), and he was doing in prison just what he had done when he was free. Preaching the gospel—and longing and praying for doors to be opened so that he could go through them and preach to people who had never heard the good news.

That was what he wanted the Colossians to pray for him: 'that God will open to us a door for the word, that we may declare the mystery of Christ'. God heard their prayers and gave them what they asked for—but in a way they could never have dreamed of. The letters Paul wrote from his prison cell spread the word far more widely than if he had gone from place to place preaching it. Those letters, which make up half the New Testament, have travelled through the world and through the years. They are reaching us this present moment— you as you read and me as I write. I find myself thinking (with tears in my eyes) about Paul in his prison cell, with his passion for Christ—sending us a letter across the years to tell us about the glory of Jesus Christ and to tell us how to live.

A final prayer

'Remember my chains', Paul wrote in his own hand... 'Grace be with you'.
So spend a few moments remembering his chains and thanking God for his life.

SB

Acts 2:1–4, 12–13 (NJB)

Pentecost

When Pentecost came round, they had all met together, when suddenly there came from heaven a sound as of a violent wind which filled the entire house in which they were sitting; and there appeared to them tongues as of fire; these separated and came to rest on the head of each of them. They were all filled with the Holy Spirit and began to speak different languages as the Spirit gave them power to express themselves. Everyone was amazed and perplexed; they asked one another what it all meant. Some, however, laughed it off: 'they have been drinking too much new wine,' they said.

Holy Spirit of God, our prayers are not usually centred on you, and yet on the Day of Pentecost it is fitting that they should be. On the Day of Pentecost the Church, or the Christian community, was born by your coming to give it life, to breathe life into this group of frightened men. You transformed them, gave them confidence in themselves and in the powers you sustained in them. From then onwards they boldly preached and confronted hostile authorities. In your power they brought the healing of the risen Christ to the sick and the needy. Conscious of your presence among them, they taught your message, made decisions in your name, sent out envoys for your task. The whole consciousness of this spreading group was alive with your power. Indeed, it was more than alive; it was bubbling and effervescing, to the extent that the onlookers thought they were drunk.

But who and what are you? You are the Paraclete whom Jesus promised to send, the Advocate who would make everything clear and lead his disciples into all truth. By you the absent Christ is made present. He promised that he would send you as his Spirit, as the Father sent him. But also it is the Father who sends you. You are the Spirit of the Father and the Spirit of the Son, in some way imparting the power, presence and authority of both Father and Son. You are the mutual love between Father and Son, who also dwells in all Christian hearts.

A prayer

Come, Holy Spirit, fill the hearts of your faithful. Enkindle in us the fire of your love.

HW

Acts 1:3–8 (NJB)

The final commission

Jesus showed himself alive to [the apostles] after his Passion by many demonstrations. For forty days he had continued to appear to them and tell them about the kingdom of God... Having met together they asked him, 'Lord, has the time come for you to restore the kingdom to Israel?' He replied, 'It is not for you to know times or dates that the Father has decided by his own authority, but you will receive the power of the Holy Spirit which will come on you, and then you will be my witnesses not only in Jerusalem, but throughout Judaea and Samaria, and indeed to earth's remotest end.'

The task of the apostles to witness needed a period of preparation after the resurrection—not surprisingly after their behaviour during the Passion. They simply ran away and deserted their Master, and there would have been a good deal of explaining and reconstruction to be done. Luke alone tells us about this conventional forty days (like the forty years of the people of Israel during the Exodus, or Elijah's forty days of preparation in the desert, or Jesus' own forty days of preparation in the desert), in which he strengthened them and confirmed their faith. This preparation was to be topped up by the coming of the Spirit of Jesus at Pentecost, without which the mission would be inconceivable.

It is striking that the preparation concentrated on the kingship (or kingdom) of God. Jesus did not preach himself, except as part of the sovereignty of God. It was the fact that God was king which remained at the centre of his message as he wished the apostles to spread it. The teaching and miracles, and even the Passion and death of Jesus, all serve to show us the facets of the kingship of God; that was the good news, and that is what the gospel teaches us today. Most of all, his resurrection shows us what it means that God is king: he raises and glorifies his beloved.

The other vital factor of the forty days is that there is no spreading of the kingship of God without a period of withdrawal in which we assimilate the message, meditate upon it and allow it to shape and transform us.

Reflect

'I am not asking you to remove them from the world. Consecrate them in the truth.'

HW

Acts 1:9–11 (NJB)

The Ascension

As he said this he was lifted up while they looked on, and a cloud took him from their sight. They were still staring into the sky as he went, when suddenly two men in white were standing beside them and they said, 'Why are you Galileans standing here looking into the sky? This Jesus who has been taken up from you into heaven will come back in the same way as you have seen him go to heaven.'

It is not easy to say what actually happened. The scene is described in terms of a 'three-decker universe', the ancient Hebrew picture of three layers, the heavens above and the underworld below the earth. This scheme of reality has long been abandoned. However, the cloud is a frequent symbol of the divine presence: Jesus has been absorbed into the divine sphere, and will be seen bodily no more. The preparation and comfort given by his bodily presence are no more; this presence of his will soon be replaced by his presence in the Spirit. This will be how he comes to and dwells in his community. The divine messengers who interpret the scene lay down the framework of the future: history has a sense and a direction. The end-point of history will be its summing up by Jesus.

The early Christians had a vivid expectation of the return of Jesus in triumph. The foremost picture of Christ painted by Paul's early letters is of the Lord who is to come again in triumph. He will take his faithful with him in a triumphal procession and submit all things to the Father. Some Christians seem even to have envisaged originally that the Second Coming would occur before any of Christ's faithful could die. Christ had literally abolished death for his followers. It was only gradually that they came to see that Christ had already come in triumph by means of his Spirit working firmly and victoriously through the Church in history. The Spirit working in the Christian community, in its leaders and in all its members will be the theme of Acts.

Reflect

'Maranatha, Come Lord Jesus' was the constant prayer of the early Christians.
HW

Acts 1:15–26 (NJB)

Judas is replaced

Peter stood up to speak... 'Brothers,' he said, 'the passage of scripture had to be fulfilled in which the Holy Spirit foretells the fate of Judas... Out of the men who have been with us the whole time that the Lord Jesus was living with us... one must be appointed to serve with us as a witness to his resurrection.' Having nominated two candidates... they prayed, 'Lord, you can read everyone's heart. Show us, therefore, which of these two you have chosen to take over this ministry and apostolate, which Judas abandoned.'... They then drew lots for them and as the lot fell to Matthias, he was listed as one of the twelve apostles.

There is often a great deal of controversy about the morality of the national lottery in Britain, and here are the foundation stones of the Church engaging in just such lottery. Well, almost! At least it is not for financial gain and it is not a gambling which can become compulsive. Choice by the lot has always been popular, in the belief that the result is guided by Fate or by the gods, or even by God.

In somewhat the same way, even with the Bible itself, Christians have often sought guidance for their actions by opening the Bible at random and letting their eyes or finger light on a phrase. This practice must be founded on a conviction that the Spirit is present at the reading of the Bible and guides that reading. In general this is a noble and praiseworthy Christian instinct. But the question is: how much we can demand miracles? Normally we may expect the Spirit to guide our reading of the Bible through enlightening our intellect, so that we understand a situation better in the light of God's word, and can then make a judgment.

The case of the choice of Matthias is unique. It is an instance of the special guidance of the Spirit in the early community. And it is important that the use of the lot comes only after the prayer of the community. A place among the Twelve is obviously unique; such an important position as one of the twelve foundation stones of the New Israel means that the community can rely on a special intervention of the Spirit.

Reflect

You did not choose me. No, I chose you, and commissioned you to go out and bear fruit.

HW

Acts 2:37–39, 41 (NJB)

The first converts

[They] said to Peter and the other apostles, 'What are we to do, brothers?' 'You must repent,' Peter answered, 'and every one of you must be baptised in the name of Jesus Christ for the forgiveness of your sins, and you will receive the gift of the Holy Spirit. The promise that was made is for you and for your children, and for all those who are far away.'… They accepted what he said and were baptised. That very day about three thousand were added to their number.

In his first proclamation at Pentecost Peter has explained the message of Jesus, and this immediately draws the first converts to commit themselves to Jesus. The Greek really means 'be baptized *into* the name of Jesus', that is, enter the company of Jesus and stand under the banner of his name.

The first condition for becoming a follower of Jesus is always, in Luke's writings, the admission that we are sinners and thus a change of heart and in our whole scale of values. The fisherman Peter is not called to his office as first of the disciples till he has cried out in the boat, 'Leave me, Lord, for I am a sinner'. The tax-collector Zacchaeus changes his ways and promises restitution before he welcomes Jesus into his house. At Calvary the good thief admits that he deserves his punishment before Jesus receives him into his Kingdom. So today the first step in many liturgies is the admission that we too are helpless sinners and need the help of Jesus.

This account also shows the first step in an exciting double movement which continues throughout Acts. On the one hand the salvation offered through the name of Jesus is seen always as the fulfilment of God's promises to Israel. Just as the Annunciations to Zechariah and to Mary are to the observant and pious faithful of Israel, so now the first converts are Jews, thus fulfilling the promises of salvation to Israel. On the other hand, time after time the Jews eventually thrust away the Christian missionaries, who then turn to others, the Gentiles, 'those who are far away'.

Reflect

So that all beings in the heavens, on the earth and in the underworld, should bend the knee at the name of Jesus.

HW

Acts 2:42–47 (NJB)

The first Christian community

These remained faithful to the teaching of the apostles, to the broth-erhood, to the breaking of bread and to the prayers. And everyone was filled with awe; the apostles worked many signs and miracles. And all who shared the faith owned everything in common; they sold their goods and possessions and distributed the proceeds among themselves according to what each one needed. Each day, with one heart, they regularly went to the Temple but met in their houses for the breaking of bread; they shared their food gladly and generously; they praised God and were looked up to by everyone. Day by day the Lord added to their community those destined to be saved.

This is the first of several summary passages in Acts in which Luke represents the Christian community of Jerusalem as the model for all Christian communities. Each element in the description is individually important, so that it is hard to give any one of them priority.

Perhaps two elements which stand out are prayer, and community of goods. Prayer is particularly important in Luke's Gospel and in Acts. In the Gospel Jesus is shown to be praying at crucial moments of his mission, before the coming of the Spirit at his baptism, at the Transfiguration, when he chooses his disciples, and again when they find him and ask to be taught how to pray like him. In imitation of their master the disciples in Acts pray before any important decision, before any new initiative in the evangelization, and when undergoing persecution. Here prayer is an important feature of their daily lives, both 'the prayers' and the formal daily

prayer in the temple. Praise of God plays an especially important part in it. It is virtually only in these summaries that the breaking of bread is mentioned, but they suggest that the eucharist was already an important part of worship.

The use of material possessions is always a tricky point for Luke. His style, imagery (banking, debts, rates of interest) and concerns show that he moved in a richer world than the agri-cultural society of Mark. It is all the more pointed that he continually warns against the misuse of wealth. Riches are perilous. The only way to avoid the dangers of wealth is use it to help those in need.

Reflect

He gives food to those who fear him,
his covenant ever in mind.

HW

53

Acts 4:1–21 (part) (NJB)

The first persecutions

While they were still talking to the people the priests came up to them, accompanied by the captain of the Temple and the Sadducees. They were extremely annoyed at their teaching the people the resurrection from the dead by proclaiming the resurrection of Jesus. They arrested them, and, as it was already late, kept them in prison till the next day. The next day the rulers held a meeting with the high priest and all the members of the high-priestly families. They made the prisoners stand in the middle and began to interrogate them, 'By what power and in whose name have you men done this?' They were astonished at the fearlessness shown by Peter and John, considering that they were une-ducated laymen. They gave them a warning on no account to teach in the name of Jesus. They could not think of any way to punish them, since all the people were giving glory to God for what had happened.

This is only the first of many times that the apostles and other messengers of Jesus will be arrested, questioned and (usually) punished. This first time they are merely cautioned. Luke stresses from the start that the history of the spread of the gospel is a continuous history of persecution. He shows how this persecution, being dragged before sanhedrins, before governors and kings, is a fulfilment of Jesus' prophecy that this would occur. It is also carefully shown to be parallel to the suffering which Jesus himself underwent. The story of the heralds and followers of Jesus is the story of his own life: they are filled with his Spirit, they continue his teaching, they work miracles like his, they are persecuted as he was. In the early part of Acts it is the apostles at Jerusalem who are so persecuted; later it is Paul. So the early community continues into the next generation the very life of Jesus.

There can seldom be a life without suffering, whether it be bereavement, handicap, dependence, misunderstanding or desertion. These were all in some measure the lot of Jesus himself. It can be an inspiration to know that as members of Christ's body our vocation is to fill out the sufferings of Christ in each generation.

Reflect

With complete fearlessness I shall go on, so that now, as always, Christ will be glorified in my body, whether by my life or by my death.

Philippians 1:20

HW

Matthew 28:16–19 (NJB)

Trinity Sunday

The eleven disciples set out for Galilee. When they saw Jesus they fell down before him, though some hesitated. Jesus came up and spoke to them. 'All authority in heaven and on earth has been given to me. Go therefore, make disciples of all nations; baptise them in the name of the Father and of the Son and of the Holy Spirit.'

O God, you inspired your Church to put this feast of the Holy Trinity at the end of the cycle of feasts. The liturgical year begins with Christmas, the sending of the Son by the Father, and his becoming man, when the Holy Spirit overshadowed Mary. Then comes the Easter group of feasts; the Son offered himself in perfect union of will to the Father, and breathed forth the Spirit. The Father raised him to new life in the Spirit. Finally at Pentecost the Father sent the Spirit of his Son to guide and inspire the community which was to carry on the Son's work on earth. Now, after all these events on earth, the Church celebrates the unchanging unity which is the beginning and goal of all action.

Lord God, we do not really know what we mean by the Trinity. No human being can see God and live. Human concepts are formed to express human situations, and can be transferred only uncomfortably beyond our human experience. For us the noblest and most valuable element in human existence is the experience of human relationships, the knowledge and love of one person for another, the vibrant communication and responsiveness of one person to another. This is what distinguishes the human world from the animal. We know that this personal relationship, this love and knowledge between persons, must exist also in you, our God, from whom we draw our origin.

All fatherhood in heaven and earth draws its name and existence from you. Human fatherhood is only the palest shadow of your Fatherhood. The relationship of a son reaches its human perfection in the loving obedience which Jesus showed on Calvary, and this too is only a shadow of the relationship of Son to Father in God. In our human language we can represent the Spirit only as the bond which binds Father and Son together.

A way to pray

The grace of the Lord Jesus Christ, the love of God and the fellowship of the Holy Spirit be with you all.

2 Corinthians 13:13

HW

Acts 6:8—7:60 (NJB)

The martyrdom of Stephen

Stephen was filled with grace and power and began to work miracles and great signs among the people. Then certain people came forward to debate with Stephen. They could not stand up against him because of his wisdom, and the Spirit that prompted what he said. But Stephen, filled with the Holy Spirit, gazed into heaven and saw the glory of God and Jesus standing at God's right hand. 'Look! I can see heaven thrown open,' he said, 'and the Son of man standing at the right hand of God.' All the members of the council shouted out and stopped their ears with their hands. Then they made a concerted rush at him, thrust him out of the city and stoned him. As they were stoning him, Stephen said in invocation, 'Lord Jesus, receive my spirit.' Then he knelt down and said aloud, 'Lord, do not hold this sin against them.' And with these words he fell asleep.

Stephen is the first to witness to Jesus with the shedding of his blood, as countless others have done since that day. This first generation of Christians continued the life of Jesus in many of its details, by their preaching, their miracles, and here by death itself. The account of the martyrdom of Stephen is designed to bring out its similarity to Jesus' passion, especially in Luke's version, even to the sight of the heavens thrown open, with the Son of man at the right hand of God, and the forgiveness of his killers.

The incident forms one of the turning-points in Acts, for Stephen's long address to the council sums up and interprets the story of the early community up to this point, and the obdurate opposition of the Jewish leaders. In this Stephen shows that they are simply following the example of their ancestors. Stephen's death also points the mission in a new direction: a persecution starts, and 'everyone except the apostles' scatters to the country districts, beginning to spread the message there. The scene now moves beyond Jerusalem—already towards 'the ends of the earth'. So here already the blood of martyrs is the seed of Christians, as Tertullian said, and as the history of Christendom would so frequently show.

Reflect

Your perseverance will win you your lives.

Luke 21:19

HW

Acts 8:4–17 (NJB)

Samaria welcomes Christ

Once they had scattered they went from place to place preaching the good news. And Philip went to a Samaritan town and proclaimed the Christ to them. The people unanimously welcomed the message Philip preached because they had heard of the miracles he worked and because they saw them for themselves. As a result there was great rejoicing in that town. When the apostles in Jerusalem heard that Samaria had accepted the word of God, they sent Peter and John to them, and they went down there and prayed for them to receive the Holy Spirit. Then they laid hands on them and they received the Holy Spirit.

Miracles and healings seem to have been just as prominent a mark of the early preaching of Christ as they were of Jesus' own mission. The presence of the Spirit was obvious in the community. So Paul, writing to the Galatians, challenges them to explain the activity of the Spirit among them as something visible and unmistakable: it cannot be the result of the Law, he claims, but can come only from Christ. Later, writing to the Corinthians, he lists the many ways in which the Spirit manifests himself. Some are extraordinary: healings, speaking in tongues, prophecy. Others are less extraordinary, but still remarkable: faith, discernment, wisdom. Still others are the more humdrum elements in a Christian life and relationship between persons, such as loyalty and perseverance. The crown of these, of course, is love. It is worth reminding ourselves that this too is demanding and cannot be taken for granted (which is why Christian marriages receive a blessing). To live all these in a Christian way requires the Spirit of Christ.

When all these manifestations of the Spirit are considered—and not only the ones which are obviously out of the ordinary—we can see how the Spirit transforms a whole personal life and a whole society. To live by the Spirit of Christ is really to live in newness of life, as a new creation.

Remarkable also is the concern for unity as the Christian community begins to spread. The unity of the little community in Jerusalem had been stressed in all the accounts of it. Now, as it expands beyond Jerusalem the apostles continue to lead and confirm the process of bringing believers to Christ and to the Spirit.

Pray

Come, Holy Spirit, fill the hearts of your faithful and kindle in us the fire of your love.

HW

Acts 8:9–22 (NJB)

Simon the magician

Now a man called Simon had for some time been practising magic arts in the town and astounded the Samaritan people. He had given it out that he was someone momentous and everyone believed in him; eminent citizens and ordinary people alike had declared, 'He is the divine power that is called Great.'... When Simon saw that the Spirit was given through the laying on of the apostles' hands, he offered them money with the words, 'Give me the same power so that anyone I lay my hands on will receive the Holy Spirit.' Peter answered, 'May your silver be lost for ever, and you with it, for thinking that money could buy what God has given for nothing! Repent of this wickedness of yours, and pray to the Lord that this scheme of yours may be forgiven.'

This incident with Simon the magician (or Magus) has given a name to 'simony', the attempt to buy spiritual advantages with money. It is an obvious and easy assumption by the rich and powerful that their wealth and their power can be used to bully God as well as men. Peter's uncompromising opposition teaches two important lessons.

Firstly, it shows the reversal of human values which has been so important throughout Luke's teaching. Jesus came to save the neglected and underprivileged. Especially in Luke's Gospel it is the outcasts of society who receive the message with joy, from the shepherds of the Nativity, through Zacchaeus the despised tax-collector, to the tortured criminal on Calvary. 'Blessed are you who are poor', and by contrast 'Woe to you who are rich'. Wealth is a hazard, which can be tamed only by the right use of wealth.

Secondly, it is impossible to bargain with God. God can receive nothing from human beings, for nothing we have to offer can make any contribution or addition to God. So God's attitude is one of pure giving, and the human attitude must be one of pure receiving. We cannot earn or merit anything from God, and any such attempt as Simon's to buy privileges from God shows a fundamental misunderstanding of the relationship of human beings to God.

Reflect

It was those who were poor according to the world that God chose, to be rich in faith and to be the heirs to the kingdom.

James 2:5

HW

Acts 8:26–38 (NJB)

The baptism of an Ethiopian

The angel of the Lord spoke to Philip saying, 'Set out at noon and go along the road that leads from Jerusalem down to Gaza, the desert road.' So he set off on his journey. Now an Ethiopian had been on pilgrimage to Jerusalem. He was [the treasurer] of the kandake, or queen, of Ethiopia... He was now on his way home; and as he sat in his chariot he was reading the prophet Isaiah. The Spirit said to Philip, 'Go up and join that chariot.' When Philip ran up he heard him reading Isaiah the prophet and asked, 'Do you understand what you are reading?' He replied, 'How could I, unless I have someone to guide me?'... Starting, therefore, with this text of scripture, Philip proceeded to explain the good news of Jesus to him. Further along the road they came to some water, and the [official] said, 'Look, here is some water; is there anything to prevent my being baptised?' He ordered the chariot to stop, then [they] both went down into the water, and [Philip] baptised him.

This story of the Ethiopian pairs well with the story of the disciples on the road to Emmaus at the end of Luke's Gospel. In each case a stranger comes up in the course of a journey and explains the message of Jesus by means of the scripture. In each case the response is enthusiastic, and instruction leads on to sacrament, the eucharistic meal or baptism. In each case the stranger then disappears inexplicably.

The lesson in each case is the same. Luke is teaching that the basic source for understanding the will of God and God's revelation is the scripture, but that this also needs interpretation according to the living voice of the Spirit in the community. In each the sacramental principle is important: the message of Christ embraces the whole person, not just the mind or the understanding. So commitment to Christ is fittingly expressed in bodily actions.

Baptism obviously symbolizes the washing away of dirt and sin, and so the cleansing of the whole person. But 'coming up out of the water' is also consistently mentioned, and Paul interprets this as rising to new life after death in Christ. By baptism the believer enters into Christ in his death and rises with him to new life.

Reflect

'Did not our hearts burn within us as he talked to us on the road and explained the scriptures to us?'

HW

Acts 9:1–8 (NJB)

The conversion of Paul

Paul went to the high priest and asked for letters addressed to the synagogues in Damascus, that would authorise him to arrest and take to Jerusalem any followers of the Way, men or women, that he might find. While he was travelling to Damascus and approaching the city suddenly a light from heaven shone all round him. He fell to the ground, and then he heard a voice saying, 'Saul, Saul, why are you persecuting me?' 'Who are you, Lord?' he asked, and the answer came, 'I am Jesus, whom you are persecuting. Get up and go into the city and you will be told what you are to do.' The men travelling with Saul stood there speechless, for though they heard the voice they could see no one. Saul got up from the ground, but when he opened his eyes he could see nothing at all, and they had to lead him into Damascus by the hand.

This splendid story of Paul on the road to Damascus is so important that it is told three times in Acts, each time with delicate variations. Is it the story of a conversion or of a vocation? The outline of the story is modelled on the conversion of Heliodorus in 2 Maccabees 3. Heliodorus, the lackey of the Syrian king Antiochus, was the arch-persecutor of God's people. But, when he came to Jerusalem to despoil the temple, he was thrown down by a supernatural force, enveloped in thick darkness, and had to be led helpless away. Thereafter the high priest prayed for his recovery, and Heliodorus returned to offer sacrifice to the Lord. Luke alludes to this story to show that in Paul's case too the persecutor of God's people is brought by heavenly means to submit to the Lord.

In other ways, however, the story is also similar to the vocation of great Old Testament figures, Abraham, Moses or Samuel. Here is a prophet being summoned by the Lord to a mission.

At the heart of the story is the perception, which occurs again and again in Paul's letters, that Christ is in each of his followers. To be a follower of Christ is to live with his life: what is done to a Christian is done to Christ.

Reflect

Christ will be glorified in my body, whether by my life or by my death. Life to me, of course, is Christ.

HW

Acts 9:10–20 (NJB)

Paul's mission begins

There was a disciple in Damascus called Ananias, and he had a vision in which the Lord said to him, 'Ananias!' When he replied, 'Here I am, Lord,' the Lord said, 'Get up and go to Straight Street and ask at the house of Judas for someone called Saul who comes from Tarsus. At this moment he is praying, and has seen a man called Ananias coming in and laying hands on him to give him back his sight. This man is my chosen instrument to bring my name before gentiles and kings and before the people of Israel.' Then Ananias went. He entered the house and laid his hands on Saul and said, 'Brother Saul, I have been sent by the Lord Jesus, who appeared to you on your way here, so that you may recover your sight and be filled with the Holy Spirit.' It was as though scales fell away from his eyes, and immediately he was able to see again. After he had spent only a few days with the disciples in Damascus, he began preaching in the synagogues, 'Jesus is the Son of God.'

The completion of the preparation of Paul for his mission is announced with the very special emphasis of a complementary vision: Ananias is shown Saul and Saul is shown Ananias. Paul is to be the apostle of the gentiles, breaking the bounds of Judaism.

Here again—as in the earlier case of the Ethiopian—the sacramental principle is in action. Saul is prepared for his mission not simply by heavenly means but also by human means: to the supernatural scene on the road to Damascus is added the human means of Ananias laying hands on Saul. The Christian community is essentially a human entity, though living with a divine life, and it works through human means, using human instruments. God prefers to use human beings as his instruments, and each of us has a task to do.

The message which Paul preaches in Damascus is the message which will be central in his letters. The introduction to Romans concerns God's Son, 'who was born a descendant of David and was designated Son of God in power by the resurrection from the dead'. The adoption of Christians as sons of God and co-heirs with Christ is a central and recurrent feature of his thought.

Reflect

God has sent into our hearts the Spirit of his Son, crying 'Abba, Father'.

Galatians 4:6

HW

1 Peter 2:4–7 (NIV)

The living temple

As you come to him, the living Stone—rejected by men but chosen by God and precious to him—you also, like living stones, are being built into a spiritual house to be a holy priesthood, offering spiritual sacrifices acceptable to God through Jesus Christ. For in Scripture it says: 'See, I lay a stone in Zion, a chosen and precious cornerstone, and the one who trusts in him will never be put to shame.' Now to you who believe, this stone is precious. But to those who do not believe, 'The stone the builders rejected has become the capstone,' and, 'A stone that causes men to stumble and a rock that makes them fall.'

We can all mix metaphors at times, and obviously St. Peter is no exception. In this chapter, Christians have been told that they are like babies, who should long for spiritual 'milk' (v. 2). Now they are told that they are to be 'living stones' in the new Temple of God. It's hard to think of a greater contradiction than a *living* stone! Stones are solid, inert, insensitive objects. But perhaps the writer had in mind his own God-given nickname, *Peter*, the rock or stone—and he was very definitely alive. So was Jesus, the utterly reliable, rock-like source of faith. So perhaps stone, or rock, isn't a bad image for the living people who make up this new building, the temple 'made without hands'. The Church is *people*, not bricks and mortar, however beautiful—a truth we forget at our peril!

In the new temple Jesus is the 'chief' stone, the one who holds the whole thing together. Although his own people failed to recognize this, he fulfilled a great prophecy of the Hebrew Scriptures. Isaiah had spoken of 'the Lord Almighty' as a 'stone' over which the people of Jerusalem would trip and be broken (Isaiah 8:14–15). Now the 'living Stone' had arrived, and they had indeed stumbled over him, like a stone rejected by the builders as not being good enough for their splendid new building! But God had destined him to be the head stone, the high 'capstone' that holds it all together.

And the great privilege is that we, who believe in him, are also 'living stones' in that new temple. No longer is God's temple a thing of stone, wood and metal, a silent, lifeless shrine, but a living community of those who put their trust in him.

A reflection

May we grow into Christ's likeness, and, made one by God's Spirit, become a living temple to his glory.

ASB

DW

Isaiah 48:17–19, 22 (NIV)

God's 'if only'

This is what the Lord says—your Redeemer, the Holy One of Israel: 'I am the Lord your God, who teaches you what is best for you, who directs you in the way you should go. If only you had paid attention to my commands, your peace would have been like a river, your righteousness like the waves of the sea. Your descendants would have been like the sand, your children like its numberless grains; their name would never be cut off nor destroyed from before me.'... 'There is no peace,' says the Lord, 'for the wicked.'

'If only' is one of those awful phrases people constantly quote when things have gone wrong. 'If only I'd had the car serviced', 'If only I'd gone to the doctor when the pain first started', 'If only I'd checked up on his credentials before going into a partnership with him'—the examples are endless. And it's all so futile! 'If only' means we didn't! Empty regrets about things we can't possibly change are simply destructive.

But God's 'if only's aren't like that. God wasn't asking his people for futile regrets about the past, but for true repentance. He wanted them to learn from their mistakes. Of course it was true that if they had not ignored his commands all the calamities that had come their way would not have befallen them. Yet even now they had the chance to learn the painful lesson: 'God knows best! I am the Lord your God who teaches you *what is best for you.*'

In other words, God's commandments aren't arbitrary instructions dreamt up to keep us under. They are the loving guidance of our redeemer, the one who wants to lead us in good paths, paths of peace.

It's a lesson children have to learn about parental guidance. When mum or dad says 'Don't play with fire' they're not being spoil-sports! Their commands are for our good—and usually, slowly but surely, we come to understand that. So is the moral law of God. If there is 'no peace for the wicked'—and experience tells us how true *that* is—then conversely true peace and true prosperity—spiritual health—flow from a joyful acceptance that God's will is best for us.

A reflection

When I am tempted to find God's standards and requirements arbitrary and irksome, let me remember that following them leads to 'peace like a river'.

DW

Isaiah 49:1–4 (NIV)

Satisfied in his hands

Listen to me, you islands; hear this, you distant nations: Before I was born the Lord called me; from my birth he has made mention of my name. He made my mouth like a sharpened sword, in the shadow of his hand he hid me; he made me into a polished arrow and concealed me in his quiver. He said to me, 'You are my servant, Israel, in whom I will display my splendour.' But I said, 'I have laboured to no purpose; I have spent my strength in vain and for nothing. Yet what is due to me is in the Lord's hand, and my reward is with my God.'

There can't be many of us who haven't, at some time or other, felt like God's Servant in this reading. 'I have laboured to no purpose.' It's as true in Christian work as in ordinary life—the youth group who have driven us to despair, the special service that hardly anyone came to, the jumble sale that cost a lot of time and energy and raised just a few pounds. Ministers know it, of course, especially those who have worked for years in hard and unpromising soil, trying to plant seed in stony or hard ground. But so do the rest of us! There's nothing exclusive about disappointment!

The contrast here is between the grandeur of God's call and the bleak reality of its consequences. The Lord gave his Servant an early call—'before I was born'—and the gift of eloquence. He promised to 'display his splendour' through his Servant, yet the actual result fell rather short of that. What should the Servant make of it? Had he mistaken the call? Had he bitten off more than he could chew? Was he deluded in his belief that God was with him?

The answers, of course, are 'No,' 'No' and 'No'! That is the lesson the Servant—and all God's servants—must learn. As it says, 'What is due to me is in the Lord's hand.' When God calls, he makes his calling clear, and he supports it with the necessary gifts and strength. All that is required of the Servant is *faithfulness*. The rewards for his work may not be evident now, but they are 'with God'—they are in God's hands, not ours. It's not an easy lesson, and most of us will go on struggling with it until all becomes clear at the judgment seat of Christ.

A reflection

When I am discouraged, may I remember that when God called me he put me 'in the shadow of his hand'. That is not a place for dissatisfaction or discouragement! All that comes to me is from those same hands, hands of faithfulness and love.

DW

Isaiah 49:5, 6 (NIV)

Light for the Gentiles

And now the Lord says—he who formed me in the womb to be his servant to bring Jacob back to him and gather Israel to himself, for I am honoured in the eyes of the Lord and my God has been my strength—he says: 'It is too small a thing for you to be my servant to restore the tribes of Jacob and bring back those of Israel I have kept. I will also make you a light for the Gentiles, that you may bring my salvation to the ends of the earth.'

Perhaps this reading should begin with 'but' rather than 'and', because it follows on from yesterday's passage. The Servant was expressing his disappointment that his work had not yet been blessed, feeling that his labour had been 'to no purpose'. 'But' the Lord has a different view of things! He had been called (as we saw yesterday) from 'before he was born'. Now it is put even more starkly. God 'formed him in the womb to be his servant'—and his servant for a particular purpose: 'to bring Jacob back to him and gather Israel to himself'. That's the size of the task, it had been assumed.

But that's 'too small a thing'—even though, up to now, it had seemed completely beyond the Servant. Now the task was to be increased—he is also to be 'a light for the Gentiles', so that God's salvation would be known 'to the ends of the earth'. At the same time, though, a deeper understanding seems to be given to him: 'My God has been my strength'. The task might seem too difficult even for the most gifted and willing human servant, but it was not too great for God.

The tasks God gives us are not shaped to our ability, but to his power. If he calls us to do something in his name, he will provide the necessary strength. That doesn't mean that the task will be easy. It doesn't guarantee immediate success. But it does mean that God *takes responsibility for it*. In a very real sense, it's not our worry any longer!

A reflection

What Isaiah needed most of all was not a job he could cope with, but faith in the God with whom 'nothing is impossible'. As we face the tasks God has given us to do—great or small— the same truth applies. 'My grace is sufficient for you, for my grace is perfected in weakness' (2 Corinthians 12:9). It's not the size of the task, but the greatness of God that is the issue. Instead of shrinking from the first, we should be putting our faith in the second!

DW

Isaiah 49:13–16 (NIV)

The God who never forgets

Shout for joy, O heavens; rejoice, O earth; burst into song, O mountains! For the Lord comforts his people and will have compassion on his afflicted ones. But Zion said, 'The Lord has forsaken me, the Lord has forgotten me.' 'Can a mother forget the baby at her breast and have no compassion on the child she has borne? Though she may forget, I will not forget you! See, I have engraved you on the palms of my hands; your walls are ever before me.'

It used to amuse me, when I was a radio producer, to watch the sound engineers marking settings and levels on their palms. It all seemed a bit pre-electronic! But, as one explained to me, 'You can lose a bit of paper, but you're not likely to lose a hand, are you?' So there it was, vital technical information for a live broadcast, written in biro on a (sometimes rather sweaty) palm!

It's an image used here, though God writes with something more permanent than biro—he 'engraves' his *aide-memoire* on the palms of his hands. And what is it that he thus engraves? The names and details of his people! Zion (Jerusalem) was afraid that God would, or even *had*, forgotten it—that its people were abandoned and forsaken. But that was not possible. The strongest of all human ties, that of a mother for her baby, is invoked as a comparison. Yes, she might, just *might* forget 'the baby at her breast', but God will not forget them. And the proof is the message

'engraved' on his palm as a constant and conspicuous reminder of his promise. The word used for 'engraved' is often associated with architect's plans. Jerusalem and its people are part of God's plan, and like a good architect he's working closely to it. It is his *purpose*, like the architect's drawing, which serves as a constant reminder of the needs of his people. No wonder they were told to 'shout for joy' and 'burst into song'. Far from being forgotten, they were in the heart of his purposes.

A reflection

There is a universal truth here—the safest place to be is in the centre of God's purpose. That's as true for God's new covenant people as it was for the people of Zion 2,500 years ago. God does not forget, but bears 'on his palm' a constant reminder of his plan for us.

DW

Isaiah 50:4–7 (NIV)

The sustaining word

The Sovereign Lord has given me an instructed tongue, to know the word that sustains the weary. He wakens me morning by morning, wakens my ear to listen like one being taught. The Sovereign Lord has opened my ears, and I have not been rebellious; I have not drawn back. I offered my back to those who beat me, my cheeks to those who pulled out my beard; I did not hide my face from mocking and spitting. Because the Sovereign Lord helps me, I will not be disgraced. Therefore have I set my face like flint, and I know I will not be put to shame.

What can sustain the believer in times of testing? That is the question answered here. The Lord's servant is being called upon to suffer ridicule and abuse—even physical violence. Yet he does not 'draw back', indeed he sets his face 'like flint'. What is the source of this strength?

The answer is in the first two sentences. An 'instructed tongue' is the tongue of one who has been taught. That's to say, what he speaks comes from someone other than himself—the Lord, clearly. So the 'word that sustains the weary' is the word of the Lord, God's message which he not only 'knows' but also shares with others. But the 'Word of the Lord' doesn't enter our hearts and minds by accident! We have to be awake and we have to listen 'like one being taught'.

The picture offered by the prophet is probably of school, or of a 'study group' gathered around a teacher. The best time to study in a hot land is early in the morning, so the students rise early and attend to the teacher's words. And they listen 'like one being taught' with the attention and concentration and application of those who actually *want* to learn.

The lesson for us is pretty clear. If we are to be 'sustained by the Word of God' we, too, will have to make time to listen to it, and when we do we shall need to give it the attention, concentration and application that we would give to a vital lesson in (say) child care or first aid. To be honest, it's all a matter of priorities. God gives us strength through his Word, but we have to be open to it.

A reflection

In times of testing I may be tempted to turn away from the Word of God, at the very moment when I most need to know 'the word that sustains the weary'.

DW

Isaiah 51:1–3 (NIV)

Listen—and look!

Listen to me, you who pursue righteousness and who seek the Lord:
Look to the rock from which you were cut and to the quarry from
which you were hewn; look to Abraham, your father, and to Sarah,
who gave you birth. When I called him he was but one, and I blessed
him and made him many. The Lord will surely comfort Zion and will
look with compassion on all her ruins; he will make her deserts like
Eden, her wastelands like the garden of the Lord. Joy and gladness
will be found in her, thanksgiving and the sound of singing.

When God's people were tempted to doubt him, they were told to *listen* to him and to *look* to 'the rock from which they were hewn'. In other words, present assurance should flow from past blessing. The God who had blessed their forebears—Abraham and Sarah—would similarly bless them, because they were cut from the same 'quarry': they were part of the same 'rock'—a 'chip off the old block', as we used to say.

So what should God's people of the *new* covenant do in similar circumstances? After all, we aren't descendants of Abraham and Sarah. We're 'chips' off a very different racial 'block'.

St Paul gives us the answer. Abraham is the 'father' of all who *believe* (see Romans 4:1–12). It was not enough for people to claim that they were 'descendants of Abraham'. They had to share Abraham's faith in God. Under the new covenant all, of any race or culture, were welcome in God's family, on the grounds of *faith*.

And that faith *listens* and *looks*, just as the Lord called the people of Jerusalem to listen and look in Isaiah's day. We listen to his promises and look at what has happened in the past. We are hewn from an even richer quarry of faith: we have Jesus and the apostles, as well as Abraham and Sarah, as our antecedents. As we listen to God and look to their example of faith, Eden will truly be restored. There will be 'thanksgiving and the sound of singing'.

A reflection

*When things are difficult and faith is
at a low ebb, it's often hard to
remember the ways God has blessed us
in the past. But he is the same God.
His love is 'steadfast'. His promises
are trustworthy. However far the rock
travels from the quarry, it's still hewn
from the same source!*

DW

John 15:9–11 (NRSV)

Complete joy

As the Father has loved me, so I have loved you; abide in my love. If you keep my commandments, you will abide in my love, just as I have kept my Father's commandments and abide in his love. I have said these things to you so that my joy may be in you, and that your joy may be complete.

The devoted lover gazed into the eyes of his beloved. 'I'd do anything for you,' he breathed. 'Your wish is my command.' And so she asks for a box of chocolates in the middle of the night, or invites him to jump off Magdalen Bridge in Oxford on May Day, or names the day of the wedding! It's absolutely normal to want to demonstrate our love for someone by doing what they want, rather than what we want.

Jesus asked his disciples to demonstrate their love for him by keeping his commandments—the newest of which, they had just learned, was to 'love one another' (13:34). He had already told them that those who love him will 'keep his word' (14:23). But he wasn't asking them to do what he had not already done himself. He had kept his Father's commandments and consequently abided in his love. It's not really possible to claim you love someone and then constantly go against their wishes. Conversely, to align ourselves completely with someone else's will is to demonstrate our perfect love for them.

In human relationships that might be rather risky! What the 'beloved' demands might not be right, or even for their true good. But where the Father and Jesus are concerned, we can be confident that what they command will be both right and for our ultimate good. Indeed, the consequence of keeping their commandments is that we 'abide' in them—rest or reside or dwell in them—and the joy of Jesus resides in us, and our joy will be 'complete'. The Greek word speaks of 'fullness'—those who do what Jesus requires will be *filled* with joy, *his* joy.

A reflection

Think for a moment of the sheer joy we can experience by making someone we love truly happy. And then apply that to your relationship to the Father and to Jesus Christ. To do what God wills for us is not slavery, but freedom to be the people he intends us to be. And the clue to that joy is 'abiding' in Christ's love. The closer we are to him the easier it will be to do what he 'commands'.

DW

Isaiah 51:4–6 (NIV)

One thing lasts for ever

Listen to me, my people; hear me, my nation: The law will go out from me; my justice will become a light to the nations. My righteousness draws near speedily, my salvation is on the way, and my arm will bring justice to the nations. The islands will look to me and wait in hope for my arm. Lift up your eyes to the heavens, look at the earth beneath; the heavens will vanish like smoke, the earth will wear out like a garment and its inhabitants die like flies. But my salvation will last for ever, my righteousness will never fail.

These words are addressed to 'the nation', that is, to Israel/Judah, God's people. Although they are at that moment still awaiting release from foreign captivity, God wants to assure them that his justice and righteousness have not been defeated. Far from it—his law and justice will one day be a 'light' for the whole world, including the heathen nations who have so troubled and tormented his chosen people. His 'salvation' and 'justice' are 'on the way'. They must not lose hope!

The key words are those two abstract nouns: justice and righteousness. They are absolutely vital words in the Old Testament, and we can't begin to understand who God is and what his purposes are until we have begun to understand what they mean. 'Justice' is based on God's *rule*. Like a good king, he is concerned that justice should be done, which means that people will answer for their actions to him. Evil must be punished; good must be recognized and rewarded.

Those are fundamental principles of justice.

'Righteousness' means, quite simply, 'doing what God requires'. Its opposite is not so much 'evil' as 'disobedience'. The 'righteous' person trusts in and obeys God, recognizing that he is the source of all goodness.

Together, justice and righteousness add up to 'salvation' (v. 6), which in biblical language is 'wholeness', true health. Without them there can be no healthy society—nor a truly 'healthy' individual. And that 'wholeness' is eternal—when even the universe ends, God's holiness and salvation will remain. They 'last for ever'.

A reflection

In the end, only God's justice, righteousness and salvation really matter. All the rest is temporary.

DW

Isaiah 51:9–11 (NIV)

The end of sorrow

Awake, awake! Clothe yourself with strength, O arm of the Lord; awake, as in days gone by, as in generations of old. Was it not you who cut Rahab to pieces, who pierced that monster through? Was it not you who dried up the sea, the waters of the great deep, who made a road in the depths of the sea so that the redeemed might cross over? The ransomed of the Lord will return. They will enter Zion with singing; everlasting joy will crown their heads. Gladness and joy will overtake them, and sorrow and sighing will flee away.

One of those odd sayings I learnt from my early childhood was 'Once bitten, twice shy'—you learn by painful experience. Most of us have got plenty of examples to back up that rather negative warning—'bargains' that weren't, short-cuts that took twice as long, purchases by 'easy payments' that turned out to be very expensive ... and difficult! One of the great themes of the Old Testament is that Israel *didn't* learn by their mistakes, they simply went on making them.

But there's another, equally valid truth of human experience, even though it doesn't seem to have got enshrined in a 'saying'. You could put it like this: 'Once blessed, twice sure'. When we've had a good experience of someone, or something, we're more confident about them, or it, next time. It applies to shops, repair men, doctors, midwives, hotels, camp-sites—almost anything, really: 'Once blessed, twice sure'.

And this is also a great biblical theme. On the evidence of the past, God's people should be able to trust him for the future. The one who 'dried up the sea'—the Red Sea, of course, at the exodus hundreds of years before—has *proved* his care for them. On the basis of past experience they can surely trust him for the future?

So the prayer goes up: 'O arm of the Lord, awake, as in days gone by'. All that is needed for the rejoicing to start is for the Lord to do again what he has done so marvellously in the past. It was not then, and should not be for us now, a prayer of doubt, but of faith. 'We'll praise him for all that is past, and trust him for all that's to come.'

A reflection

God does not change. What he has done, he can still do. That is a truth to hold to in times of testing.

DW

Isaiah 51:12–15 (NIV)

A word to the fearful

'I, even I, am he who comforts you. Who are you that you fear mortal men, the sons of men, who are but grass, that you forget the Lord your Maker, who stretched out the heavens and laid the foundations of the earth, that you live in constant terror every day because of the wrath of the oppressor, who is bent on destruction? For where is the wrath of the oppressor? The cowering prisoners will soon be set free; they will not die in their dungeon, nor will they lack bread. For I am the Lord your God, who churns up the sea so that its waves roar—the Lord Almighty is his name.'

It's all very well being told not to be scared of people! Most of us are scared of *somebody*—a boss, or a neighbour, or even someone we love very dearly but we're terrified of 'upsetting' them. It's a fact of life that most of us are sometimes very fearful of our fellow mortals—much more fearful of them than we are of God, in fact!

That was the position of the people of Jerusalem to whom the prophet speaks these words in the name of God. Of course, they had much more reason to 'fear' mortal men than most of us do. After all, they were under a cruel and brutal occupying force, and were liable to severe punishment, even death, for standing firm for their faith. The armed soldiers seemed rather more *immediate* than the invisible presence of the God of comfort.

But that was the lesson they needed to learn. They were *too* aware of the power and presence of the enemy, and forgetful of the power and presence of their Maker—the one who 'stretched out the heavens and laid the founda-

tions of the earth'. After all, the oppressors were also just mortals like themselves—'but grass', which in the Middle East soon scorches away in the noonday sun. Why were they so impressed by what was fleeting and transient, and so reluctant to trust the One who is eternal and unchanging?

It's a question we might ask ourselves! Getting things in perspective is one of the keys to a balanced and happy life, but we all know it's easier said than done.

A reflection

Before facing the day, with all its real and imaginary terrors, perhaps we should try to spend a few moments contemplating the infinite power of God—the 'Lord Almighty', the one who 'comforts you'. The people who terrify us are mortal, as we are. So why do we take more notice of them than of the Creator of 'all that is, seen and unseen'?

DW

Isaiah 53:2b–5 (NIV)

True beauty

He had no beauty or majesty to attract us to him, nothing in his appearance that we should desire him. He was despised and rejected by men, a man of sorrows, and familiar with suffering. Like one from whom men hide their faces he was despised, and we esteemed him not. Surely he took up our infirmities and carried our sorrows, yet we considered him stricken by God, smitten by him, and afflicted. But he was pierced for our transgressions, he was crushed for our iniquities; the punishment that brought us peace was upon him, and by his wounds we are healed.

Nothing attractive, nothing beautiful, nothing majestic, nothing desirable— *except what he did*. That's the message of these very familiar verses. They describe the Lord's 'Suffering Servant', and Christians have from earliest times seen in them a description of the ultimate 'Suffering Servant', the Son of God, who loved us and gave himself for us.

It's a lesson in values. The world places enormous store by outward appearance. What matters is what we look like—beauty and attractiveness; or the power and influence we wield— majesty. In modern politics, for instance, an attractive appearance on television seems to be worth more than oceans of integrity or wisdom. We say 'appearances are deceptive', but we don't appear to live by it. And many people are made miserable because they believe themselves to be unattractive or undesirable.

Yet it was this person who was 'despised and rejected by men', who did everything for us. This unattractive, uncharismatic figure took up our weaknesses, carried our sorrows, suffered for our sins and brought us peace and healing through his wounds.

There is surely a message here for all who feel that they are 'undesirable' or 'unattractive'. True beauty, true worth lies much deeper than outward appearance. As the prophet Samuel told Jesse, when he rejected his older, handsome sons when selecting David to be anointed as future king (1 Samuel 16:7), 'Man looks at the outward appearance, but the Lord looks at the heart'. There is a beauty in sacrificial service and burden-bearing which is more real and more lasting than skin-deep 'attractiveness'.

A reflection

Help me to look deeper than the surface in valuing others, and to value myself in God's terms rather than the world's.

DW

Isaiah 53:6, 7 (NIV)

The silent witness

We all, like sheep, have gone astray, each of us has turned to his own way; and the Lord has laid on him the iniquity of us all. He was oppressed and afflicted, yet he did not open his mouth; he was led like a lamb to the slaughter, and as a sheep before her shearers is silent, so he did not open his mouth.

There is something almost superhuman about silence when we are under unjustified attack! Every human instinct urges us to justify ourselves, to 'stand up for our rights', to fight our 'corner'. And that's as true in church life as it is at work, school, factory or club.

Yet here we have a picture of the totally innocent 'Servant of the Lord', whose only 'crime' is that he was bearing the sins and iniquities of others, remaining silent before his accusers, offering not a single word in his own defence. As we read the words, we are reminded of Jesus, who—according to Matthew and Mark—remained silent before his accusers, only speaking when asked directly whether he was in fact the Messiah. Indeed, in all four Gospels he offers at no point any 'defence' of his actions. It was as though he were saying, 'Let what I have done speak for me'.

Over the years I have often felt that I have been unfairly treated, or my words or actions unjustly criticized. Generally speaking, I have, I'm afraid, 'given as good as I've got'. The result has seldom been what I had hoped, with opponents collapsing in confusion, admitting that I was right all along! On the other hand, I have seen occasions when people have declined to get drawn into confrontation and self-justification, where reconciliation and healing have followed.

The way of Christ is not the way of self-justification. We are 'justified by faith in Christ', as St Paul says (Romans 5:1), not by our own arguments and excuses. Of course, truth sometimes demands that we should counter lies and calumnies—preferably those directed at others rather than ourselves. But there is a God-given gift of silence that can make all the difference to a scene of conflict. As the saying goes, 'Least said, soonest mended!'

A reflection

'When they hurled their insults at him, he did not retaliate; when he suffered, he made no threats. Instead, he entrusted himself to him who judges justly' (1 Peter 2:23). That was how the apostle describes the response of Jesus to unfair and unjust attack.

DW

Isaiah 53:9–12 (NIV)

Suffering, but satisfied

He was assigned a grave with the wicked, and with the rich in his death, though he had done no violence, nor was any deceit in his mouth. Yet it was the Lord's will to crush him and cause him to suffer, and though the Lord makes his life a guilt offering, he will see his offspring and prolong his days, and the will of the Lord will prosper in his hand. After the suffering of his soul, he will see the light [of life] and be satisfied; by his knowledge my righteous servant will justify many, and he will bear their iniquities. Therefore I will give him a portion among the great, and he will divide the spoils with the strong, because he poured out his life unto death, and was numbered with the transgressors. For he bore the sin of many, and made intercession for the transgressors.

This is a strange passage, full of complex ideas and textual problems! Scholars battle over the meaning of the text, with the result that you can find half a dozen different interpretations of it. Yet the basic idea is one that runs like a silver stream through the Scriptures—to do God's will, even if it involves suffering and sacrifice, is the only way to true life and satisfaction. That is what the 'Suffering Servant' did. That is what Jesus Christ did. It is the path of God's will, that looks beyond the present to the eternal.

The contrast is found all through these verses. On the one hand, it is apparently 'the Lord's will to crush' his Servant—indeed, to 'cause him to suffer'. The Lord will use his life as a 'guilt offering'—like the sacrifices of lambs and goats in the temple. Yet 'he will see his offspring and prolong his days'; in his hand 'the will of the Lord will prosper'; and after he has suffered he will 'see the light of life and be satisfied'. In other words, by his obedience he will not only bring forgiveness to others, but joy to himself. He will 'divide the spoils with the strong', like a victor in a battle, and will receive the kind of rewards given to the great and powerful.

If all of that sounds very complicated and remote from everyday experience, then let the words of an old chorus express it rather more simply!
Trust and obey, for there's no other way To be happy in Jesus, but to trust and obey!

A reflection

If God's will for us seems hard, to be outside it is far, far worse.

DW

Galatians 3:25–28 (NRSV)

All one in Christ Jesus

But now that faith has come, we are no longer subject to a disciplinarian, for in Christ Jesus you are all children of God through faith. As many of you as were baptized into Christ have clothed yourselves with Christ. There is no longer Jew or Greek, there is no longer slave or free, there is no longer male or female; for all of you are one in Christ Jesus.

In the ancient world of Paul's time there were three enormous barriers separating people off from each other. There was the barrier of race, tall enough in ordinary cases but infinitely high in the case of the Jews, who regarded Gentiles ('Greeks', here) almost as another species. There was the barrier of slavery, which separated 'free' men and women from those in bondage to masters; and there was the barrier of sex, which divided men (who were in charge) from women (who weren't!).

In the whole history of the ancient world, no society had breached those barriers. They seemed immovable and absolute. Jews and Gentiles were separate and different; so were freemen and slaves; so were men and women. It took the revolutionary impact of the Christian Gospel to break down the walls, but when it did, it did it *totally*.

The key to the revolution was baptism. If, in baptism, the believer was united to Christ—became one with him, 'clothed with Christ', in Paul's language here—then all other distinctions were automatically abolished. A Jew became united to Christ, so how was he different from a Gentile united to Christ? A slave became one with Christ, and by that action became identical to a freeman united to Christ. A woman 'in Christ' and a man 'in Christ' were thereby made one with each other. How could there be these human distinctions any longer? They were new people; they were 'in Christ'.

Paul doesn't say each of these different groups should be treated differently, or better. He simply says the distinctions exist no longer. 'In Christ *there is no longer* Jew or Greek, slave or free, men or women.' The world had heard nothing like it before. Sadly, it has taken many centuries for Christians themselves to take on board all its vast implications.

A reflection

The truth that distinctions of race, social standing and gender are abolished in Christ doesn't mean that we cannot celebrate the wonder of human difference!

DW

Isaiah 54:5–8 (NIV)

Married to our maker

'For your Maker is your husband—the Lord Almighty is his name—the Holy One of Israel is your Redeemer; he is called the God of all the earth. The Lord will call you back as if you were a wife deserted and distressed in spirit—a wife who married young, only to be rejected,' says your God. 'For a brief moment I abandoned you, but with deep compassion I will bring you back. In a surge of anger I hid my face from you for a moment, but with everlasting kindness I will have compassion on you,' says the Lord your Redeemer.

While it's not an uncommon idea in Jewish thought that Israel is the Lord's 'bride', the idea is seldom expressed as powerfully as it is here. 'Your Maker is your husband' is an astonishing claim—that the One who created us could be in the most intimate of all personal relationships with those he has made! The same concept is picked up in the New Testament, of course, with the Church, the people of the new covenant, described as being 'the bride of Christ'.

But the point of the analogy here goes even further than simply claiming an intimate relationship between God and his people. For in this 'marriage' one partner, the wife (us, as it were), has been rejected and deserted. Of course, God has not done this because he prefers someone else, but because of the continual unfaithfulness of the 'wife'. He did it, we read, 'in a surge of anger', but only 'for a brief moment'. Now, with 'deep compassion', he is ready to 'bring her back'.

The idea encapsulates much of the story of the Bible, in both Testaments. Israel had forfeited her claim to be 'married' to the Lord, yet in his mercy he gave her 'another chance'. He was not willing to see his chosen 'bride' abandoned and deserted, no matter how deserved was her fate. In the story of the coming of Jesus we have a similar picture. Though the whole human race had fallen into sin, 'while we were still sinners Christ died for us' (Romans 5:8)—in order to make the people of this 'new covenant' his 'bride'. Both pictures speak of God's infinite patience and mercy. He wants us to know and love him, and always takes the initiative in welcoming back his weak and faithless 'partners'.

A reflection

God does not reject us. We may reject him, but in patient love he longs for us to return.

DW

Isaiah 55:1–3 (NIV)

Something for nothing

Come, all you who are thirsty, come to the waters; and you who have no money, come, buy and eat! Come, buy wine and milk without money and without cost. Why spend money on what is not bread, and your labour on what does not satisfy? Listen, listen to me, and eat what is good, and your soul will delight in the richest of fare. Give ear and come to me; hear me, that your soul may live. I will make an everlasting covenant with you, my faithful love promised to David.

This is the language of the street market! 'Look at this offer! Something for nothing! Wine and milk absolutely free!' Who could resist such a bargain? It's an offer from someone who is rich to those who are poor, because clearly *someone* has got unlimited supplies of food and drink. Yet the appeal is to those who have 'no money'. There's a lovely paradox, too: what does it mean to 'buy' wine and milk 'without cost'? Surely that's a strange piece of business?

It is a marvellous picture of what the Bible calls 'grace'—undeserved, unearned favour. In fact, nowhere is the idea conveyed so vividly. Here is a market stall, loaded with all God's best gifts—life-sustaining water, the sparkling wine of joy, the milk that builds up our strength. And it is all on free offer! There's no way we can earn it. There is no payment we could make that would give us the right to it. Yet it is all freely available as *gift*. That is precisely what 'grace' is: what we could never deserve, we can accept as a gift from God.

Yet there is a condition, not one that would 'earn' us the good things, but one that releases them to us. We are to 'give ear and come to me', says God. If we 'listen' to him, if we 'hear' him, if we turn to him, then what his 'faithful love promised to David' will be ours. To get hold of the concept of grace is to grasp the very heart of the Christian faith. It makes sense of what we do when we hold out empty hands at the communion table and are given the gifts of God's love—at no charge!

'Only by grace can we enter; only by grace can we stand. Not by our human endeavour, but by the blood of the Lamb.' The modern worship song has got it exactly right. It is all gift!

A reflection

Our human nature will tell us that we only get what we earn or deserve. It takes a spiritual miracle for us to swallow our pride, and accept the generosity of God.

DW

Isaiah 55:6–9 (NIV)

The hour of decision

Seek the Lord while he may be found; call on him while he is near. Let the wicked forsake his way and the evil man his thoughts. Let him turn to the Lord, and he will have mercy on him, and to our God, for he will freely pardon. 'For my thoughts are not your thoughts, neither are your ways my ways,' declares the Lord. 'As the heavens are higher than the earth, so are my ways higher than your ways and my thoughts than your thoughts.'

'He who hesitates is lost.' It always seemed to me that that splendid advice was somewhat contradicted by another, equally valid proverb, 'Look before you leap.' In fact, there's no reason why they shouldn't *both* be true. There is a kind of 'hesitation' which is really born of fear or indecisiveness, and that can mean that we fail to seize opportunities in life. And there is a kind of 'leaping' to decisions which is really sheer impulsiveness, and can betray us into awful, spur of the moment decisions we live to regret. What the prophet is speaking of here is *not missing God's moments.*

It's not that God cuts us off from his love if we fail to respond to him immediately. If that were so, some of the finest Christians would be outside the kingdom! It's more a matter of recognition—of being responsive to those special times when God draws near to us in mercy or blessing. Blind Bartimaeus seized his moment when Jesus was passing through the gate of Jericho. The window of opportunity was brief, but he grasped it, shouting until he got the attention of Jesus (see Mark 10:46ff). Those who consistently turn deaf ears to the voice of God will find that it often begins to grow very faint!

Sometimes what he calls us to do in response is not at all what we might have expected! That is because our 'ways' are not 'his ways'—in other words we can't hope to understand God's 'methods of working', they're simply beyond us. But also his 'thoughts'—his intentions and purposes—are very different from ours. Indeed, they are not just different, but infinitely 'higher' ... as 'the heavens are higher than the earth'. That's why we need to be very attentive to his voice and his presence. They draw us *higher*.

A reflection

May God's thoughts draw my thoughts up from earth to heaven.

DW

Isaiah 55:10,11 (NIV)

The fertilizing word

As the rain and the snow come down from heaven, and do not return to it without watering the earth and making it bud and flourish, so that it yields seed for the sower and bread for the eater, so is my word that goes out from my mouth: It will not return to me empty, but will accomplish what I desire and achieve the purpose for which I sent it.

The biblical scholar R.N. Whybray says of this passage that it is 'the most profound statement about God's word in the Old Testament'. That suggests it's worth close attention!

As so often in Hebrew literature, it's based on a beautiful comparison. Rural people were aware of the effect of rain and snow. They weren't miserable things that spoilt holidays or blocked the roads! They were the indispensable agents of growth. Because the rain and snow fell from the skies, the fields could 'bud and flourish', which meant that the people who depended on their produce could have grain and bread. The rain and snow, in other words, were there for a purpose, and that purpose was *growth*.

So, says the Lord, is his 'word'— and by that the Bible means his declared purpose, his revealed truth. What God 'speaks'—whether through prophet, law or the inward voice of conscience—has a purpose, and that purpose, too, is growth. It is meant to multiply. 'It will not return to me empty.'

Indeed, it 'will accomplish the purpose for which I sent it'. God doesn't waste his breath! What he says happens. What he promises is fulfilled. He doesn't speak what we call 'empty words', he doesn't make empty threats or idle boasts. God's word is an effective agent of his purpose.

It was so from the beginning, for it was by God's 'word' that the universe was created. He said, 'Let there be light', and there was light—the so-called Big Bang, perhaps! Those were not idle words; and nor was his clearest 'word' of all, the Word made flesh, Jesus. Through him, too, God accomplished what he set out to do, and that was nothing less than the salvation of the world.

A reflection

If I am ever tempted to treat God's word with indifference, let me remember that he has never yet been known to fail to fulfil it!

DW

Isaiah 55:12,13 (NIV)

Paradise regained

You will go out in joy and be led forth in peace; the mountains and hills will burst into song before you, and all the trees of the field will clap their hands. Instead of the thornbush will grow the pine tree, and instead of briers the myrtle will grow. This will be for the Lord's renown, for an everlasting sign, which will not be destroyed.'

Everybody knows that Milton wrote a book called *Paradise Lost*, though hardly anyone has actually read it! Many fewer know that he also wrote *Paradise Regained*. The first book describes the Fall, with Satan as a kind of 'anti-hero'. The second tells the story of our redemption. We have had much in Isaiah about 'loss'. Now we have a song of loss redeemed.

Many scholars think these verses are the end of Second Isaiah. Whether that is so or not, they are a fitting climax to the prophet's message. All creation will join in praising the Lord's eventual triumph, when he brings his people home again. We're familiar, from the Psalms, with this lovely idea of the created order singing God's praise: 'The heavens are telling the glory of God; and the firmament proclaims his handiwork'. Here the very mountains and hills burst into song, and the trees of the field clap their hands. It's a daring and delightful picture!

Verse 13 changes the perspective. Now we are to see 'paradise regained'. In the Genesis story of 'man's first disobedience' (as Milton called it), certain 'curses' were put upon creation. The earth would bring forth thorns and thistles, so that man's labour, which had been all joy, would now be irksome and back-breaking—'in the sweat of your face you shall eat bread' (Genesis 3:19). Yet now, in the day of redemption, pine trees will replace thornbushes and myrtles replace briers. What had been sweated labour would now once again be joy.

That is what redemption means—being brought back to where we were before things went wrong. For Christians, the day of redemption is now. In Christ the 'curse' has been lifted, if we could only see it. Work and childbirth can again be joy, and the male–female relationship can again become an equal and loving partnership. No wonder the trees clap their hands!

A reflection

God's redemption has far-reaching consequences, not just for individuals, but for the whole world.

DW

Isaiah 57:15–16, 18–19 (NIV)

Above, yet near

For this is what the high and lofty One says—he who lives for ever, whose name is holy: 'I live in a high and holy place, but also with him who is contrite and lowly in spirit, to revive the spirit of the lowly and to revive the heart of the contrite. I will not accuse for ever, nor will I always be angry, for then the spirit of man would grow faint before me—the breath of man that I have created... I have seen his ways, but I will heal him; I will guide him and restore comfort to him, creating praise on the lips of the mourners in Israel. Peace, peace, to those far and near,' says the Lord. 'And I will heal them.'

A man was telling me the other day of his school days, which were made miserable for him by the attitude of his father—in other respects a loving and caring person. But nothing his son did at school was ever quite good enough. When he came home with a report showing that he'd got five 'A's and three 'A-'s, he *knew* that his father would urge him to turn those minuses into straight 'A's next term. It was all profoundly depressing! All blame, and no praise.

Some of us feel like that in our Christian experience. To have God's perfection and holiness endlessly held before us, alongside our constant failure, only causes 'the spirit of man to grow faint' before him. But the Lord doesn't want to turn us into defeatists. He 'knows that we are but dust', as the psalmist says. He has 'seen our ways' (v. 18), *yet he will heal us*.

This is as vivid a picture as we can find of the 'double' nature of God, what the theologians call his 'transcendence' and his 'immanence'. He is,

indeed, far above us. He 'lives in a high and holy place' (v. 15). That is his 'transcendence'—the word means 'over and above'—and we need to remember that he is the 'high and lofty One...who lives for ever'. But he also dwells with the person who is 'contrite and lowly in spirit' (v. 15). God will 'guide him and restore comfort to him'—not because the person is perfect, but because God understands his 'ways', and because he has a lowly and 'contrite' heart. That is God's 'immanence'—the word means 'nearness'. The One who made us loves us, and draws near to the humble and contrite.

That is the antidote to spiritual defeatism! The King of kings is our friend. Our friend is the King of kings!

A reflection

Day by day, may I appreciate that while the Lord is above me he is also and always with me.

DW

Matthew 19:16–22 (NIV)

The practical test

Now a man came up to Jesus and asked, 'Teacher, what good thing must I do to get eternal life?' 'Why do you ask me about what is good?' Jesus replied. 'There is only One who is good. If you want to enter life, obey the commandments.' 'Which ones?' the man enquired. Jesus replied, 'Do not murder, do not commit adultery, do not steal, do not give false testimony, honour your father and mother,' and 'love your neighbour as yourself.' 'All these I have kept,' the young man said. 'What do I still lack?' Jesus answered, 'If you want to be perfect, go, sell your possessions and give to the poor, and you will have treasure in heaven. Then come, follow me.' When the young man heard this, he went away sad, because he had great wealth.

Whatever way you look at it, this is a tragic little story. The man—often called 'the rich young ruler'—sounds a likeable character, sincere and honest. His claim to have kept the commandments, at any rate by the letter of the law, has the ring of truth about it. So why should Jesus demand of him what he manifestly *didn't* demand of anyone else, that he should 'sell all his possessions and give them to the poor'? He didn't ask the wealthy Nicodemus to do that, or Joseph of Arimathea, or the women among his disciples who 'supported him out of their resources'. So why this man?

The answer must lie within the inner recesses of the man's character—secret depths known only to the Son of God. It's significant, perhaps, that Jesus quoted to him the commandments that relate to our duty towards our neighbour. Indeed, he added to the end of his short list the requirement of *love* towards our neighbour, *as we love ourselves*. It may well have been that this man was a dutiful and devout Jew who kept the letter of the law scrupulously, yet by clinging to his wealth failed to honour his poor parents, perhaps, or care for the poor people who begged at his gate. There is no commandment that tells us to be generous, thoughtful, open-handed—yet the law of God is rendered void if all we do is keep to the cold requirement. What Jesus put to him—and, I suspect, often puts to us—was the *practical* test: you say you love me; well then, *show* it!

A reflection

May today's Gospel challenge me in those inner recesses of my character, where only the Lord can see. What do I cling to? Where have I held back?
DW

Mark 8:27–30 (NIV)

The key question

Jesus and his disciples went on to the villages around Caesarea Philippi. On the way he asked them, 'Who do people say I am?' They replied, 'Some say John the Baptist; others say Elijah; and still others, one of the prophets.' 'Who do you say that I am?' Peter answered, 'You are the Christ.' Jesus warned them not to tell anyone about him.

Among the invitations that bombarded us during our first few days as university students was one from a group of Christians to a Friday afternoon tea-party. After tea and some friendly chat a woman surgeon spoke to us. I remember nothing about her talk except its title: 'What do you think of Christ?' That is the pivotal question, the question Jesus asked his followers: 'Who do *you* say I am?' I had had a conventional church upbringing, and at that point in my life I could recite the creeds without disputing them but without understanding them: 'I believe... in Jesus Christ, his only Son, conceived through the Holy Spirit, born of the Virgin Mary... crucified, dead and buried... He rose again from the dead...' But my theoretical assent made little impact on my life. Three days later I made a new commitment to Jesus that revolutionized my life then and over the forty years since. If we want to concur wholeheartedly with Peter in his affirmation 'You are the Christ', there are implications for our lives; for our attitudes, our speech,

our behaviour, our decisions and our priorities. Jesus Christ, Son of the living God, deserves nothing less.

'Jesus warned them not to tell anyone about Him.' As John wrote, 'his hour had not yet come' (John 7:30). Jesus was not ready for the whole world to recognize him; his death and resurrection needed to precede the proclamation that the Messiah, the Saviour of the world, had come. The sad thing is that, nearly 2,000 years later, there appear to be many Christians who still think that they are 'not to tell anyone about him'. But the gospel is good news, exciting news. We should not keep it secret any longer!

A question to face

If Jesus were to ask you, face to face, 'Who do you say I am?' how would you reply? In what ways does your answer make a difference in your life?
RG

Mark 8:31–35 (NIV)

Death for life's sake

He then began to teach them that the Son of Man must suffer many things and be rejected by the elders, chief priests and teachers of the law, and that he must be killed and after three days rise again. He spoke plainly about this, and Peter took him aside and began to rebuke him. But when Jesus turned... he rebuked Peter. 'Get behind me, Satan!...You do not have in mind the things of God, but the things of men.' Then he... said: 'If anyone would come after me, he must deny himself and take up his cross and follow me. For whoever wants to save his life will lose it, but whoever loses his life for me and for the gospel will save it.'

Peter's motto appears to be 'Speak first, think afterwards.' Were he more cautious he might have been less ready to declare 'You are the Christ.' Peter would have been slower, too, to dispute with Jesus when he told his disciples about his suffering and death. It is easy for us, with hindsight, to criticize Peter for arguing with Jesus. We do not need to question the crucifixion; it is a fact of history. But to Peter and the others it seemed unthinkable; they were shocked to the core. They ignored the evidence of the Pharisees' hostility, plain from the start of his public ministry. They ignored the evidence of the prophets who had foretold the Messiah's death. Isaiah 53, for example, is shot through with phrases like 'a man of sorrows... familiar with suffering... a lamb to the slaughter... cut off from the land of the living... assigned a grave...' It seemed impossible that their beloved friend, whom they had just acknowledged as the Messiah, should leave them.

Jesus' perspective on life and death is topsy-turvy by the world's normal standards: death if we try to grasp life, but life through loss. It looks crazy, but that is the example he set us. I have recently stayed with a clergyman and his wife who have had to leave their congregation as a result of a power struggle with a few leading church members. But they see God teaching them and refining them through the pain; they are experiencing the truth of Jesus' words, 'who ever loses his life for me and the gospel will save it.'

A prayer

Lord, if I'm honest I like life to be comfortable. But I want to follow you; so please help me to trust you to give me strength to cope with whatever pain and suffering you allow in my life.

RG

Mark 9:2–10 (NIV)

A glimpse of glory

Jesus took Peter, James and John... and led them up a high mountain... There he was transfigured before them. His clothes became dazzling white... And there appeared before them Elijah and Moses, who were talking with Jesus. Peter said to Jesus, 'Rabbi, it is good for us to be here. Let us put up three shelters—one for you, one for Moses and one for Elijah.' (He did not know what to say, they were so frightened.) Then a cloud appeared and enveloped them, and a voice came from the cloud: 'This is my Son, whom I love. Listen to him!' Suddenly... they no longer saw anyone with them, except Jesus... Jesus gave them orders not to tell anyone what they had seen until the Son of Man had risen from the dead.

Try to put yourself in the shoes of one of the three disciples. Think of their tramp up the mountain; their thoughts about the previous conversations we have been reading; their mixed emotions as they wondered what it all meant and where Jesus was taking them. Then they watched as his appearance changed; notice that we are only told about his clothes, nothing about his face. When Moses came down from Mount Sinai with the tablets of the ten commandments 'his face was radiant because he had spoken with the Lord' (Exodus 34:29). Moses reflected God's glory; Jesus shone with his own glory.

Suddenly Jesus was joined by two figures whom they could recognize as Elijah and Moses. Peter's inept suggestion of three shelters implies that he expected the experience to last. But we cannot blame him. It is hardly surprising that they were scared; it was utterly outside their experience and comprehension. Fear brings out reactions that we realize are foolish when we look later at the situation. I find it hard to know what I would have done in the situation. What do you think would have been appropriate?

Three phrases in the passage strike me; each one could be a focus for meditation. 1 *Listen to him!* That makes a good motto for our praying and our living. 2 *They no longer saw anyone, except Jesus.* Focus on Jesus and him alone. 3 *Not to tell anyone until the Son of Man had risen.* Don't tell, until... Not 'don't tell, ever,' as we thought on Monday.

For reflection

'God has shone in our hearts to give the light of the knowledge of his glory in the face of Jesus Christ.'

2 Corinthians 4:6

RG

Mark 9:14–19 (NIV)

We can't do it!

When they came to the other disciples, they saw a large crowd around them and the teachers of the law arguing with them. As soon as all the people saw Jesus, they were overwhelmed with wonder and ran to greet him. 'What are you arguing about?' he asked. A man in the crowd answered, 'Teacher, I brought my son, who is possessed by a spirit that has robbed him of speech. Whenever it seizes him, it throws him to the ground. He foams at the mouth, gnashes his teeth and becomes rigid. I asked your disciples to drive out the spirit, but they could not.' 'O unbelieving generation,' Jesus replied, 'how long shall I stay with you? How long shall I put up with you? Bring the boy to me.'

Jesus and his three disciples came from the mountain-top experience straight into battle, a battle that had many aspects.

• A LONGRUNNING BATTLE WITH THE PHARISEES An argument was in progress between the Pharisees and Jesus' followers. The Pharisees must have been glad to show up the disciples' weakness in the situation. However hard they tried to trip Jesus up, he always got the better of them.

• A BATTLE OVER FAITH Jesus was distressed to see how the people, even his friends, still doubted God's power. This was not a battle of aggression or confrontation, but of grief. He knew that he had not got long with them; the transfiguration was a reminder that he would soon return to glory with his Father. How was he to leave them to carry on the work without him?

• AN ETERNAL BATTLE WITH EVIL The most obvious battle was with the evil spirit that triggered the fit. It was a battle that at present the disciples felt unable to face; that would change after the Holy Spirit filled them with his power on the day of Pentecost.

To think over

What are the battles in your life, both internal and external? They may be battles with circumstances, with other people, with indecision, with your own weaknesses, even with God. Pray about each one, asking God to show you what he wants you to do and how he can help you. Don't be afraid of being totally honest with him.

RG

Mark 9:20–27 (NIV)

Jesus—can you?

So they brought [the boy]. When the spirit saw Jesus, it immediately threw the boy into a convulsion. He fell to the ground and rolled around, foaming at the mouth. Jesus asked the boy's father, 'How long has he been like this?' 'From childhood,' he answered. 'It has often thrown him into the fire or water to kill him. But if you can do anything, take pity on us and help us.' ' "If you can"?' said Jesus. 'Everything is possible for him who believes.' Immediately the boy's father exclaimed, 'I do believe; help me overcome my unbelief!' ... [Jesus] rebuked the evil spirit. 'You deaf and mute spirit,' he said, 'I command you, come out of him and never enter him again.' The spirit shrieked, convulsed him violently and came out. The boy looked so much like a corpse that many said, 'He's dead.' But Jesus took him by the hand and lifted him to his feet, and he stood up.

At the heart of this story is the conversation between Jesus and the boy's father. Notice how the conversation progressed. It started with the basic facts: 'How long?'... 'From childhood.' It moved to a request: 'Please help us.' But the man was not really sure about Jesus on two counts. *Could* he heal? ('If you can...') Would he *want* to? ('Take pity...') Jesus then affirmed his power: 'Everything is possible.' It is not faith by itself that has power; 'faith' cannot exist as a separate entity. But faith reaches up to the hand of the Almighty and his power. The man responded with a wonderfully realistic prayer: 'I do believe; help me overcome my unbelief.'

Maybe we can say with Job 'I know you can do all things; no plan of yours can be thwarted' (Job 42:2). But at the same time we are confused and in pain, not understanding why God seems to be letting us down. He does not mind what emotions we throw at him; he wants our honesty. But he does not want us to be ruled by our negativity; rather to open it up to him, to allow his Spirit of love and power to flow in and change us. Like David in many of the psalms, Jeremiah demonstrates this clearly. In Lamentations chapter 3 he expresses how he feels utterly crushed by life, even by God. He pours out his pain; then he turns to say, 'Yet this I call to mind and therefore I have hope; because of the Lord's great love we are not consumed, for his compassions never fail' (Lamentations 3:21–22).

A prayer to use

Lord, I believe; help me overcome my unbelief.

RG

Mark 9:33–37 (NIV)

Who matters most?

They came to Capernaum. When he was in the house, he asked them, 'What were you arguing about on the road?' But they kept quiet because on the way they had argued about who was greatest. Sitting down, Jesus called the Twelve and said, 'If anyone wants to be first, he must be the very last, and the servant of all.' He took a little child and had him stand among them. Taking him in his arms, he said to them, 'Whoever welcomes one of these little children in my name welcomes me; and whoever welcomes me does not welcome me but the one who sent me.'

Jesus knew that the disciples had not been happy on the journey. But he waited till they were inside the house to ask them what the trouble was. And then they did not dare answer; they were ashamed, afraid of his rebuke. But he knew anyway; he always did.

I wonder who started the argument. James and John, perhaps, the 'sons of thunder', who hoped for the best seats in heaven? or Peter the impulsive, the other member of the 'inner trio'? or Judas, the group's treasurer? Whoever it was, Jesus called the whole group together, and explained how God's thinking is upside-down from ours. 'Whoever wants to be first must be last... must be the servant.' He demonstrated this truth now by putting a toddler in the centre of the room: 'If you welcome this infant you will not only welcome me but also the Father.' He demonstrated it after the last supper when he took a basin and towel to wash his disciples' feet: 'Now that I,

your Lord and Teacher, have washed your feet, you also should wash one another's feet. I have set you an example that you should do as I have done to you' (John 13:14,15). And he demonstrated it supremely on the cross: he 'did not consider equality with God something to be grasped, but... he humbled himself and became obedient to death—even death on a cross!' (Philippians 2:6–8)

To think over

As we look at Jesus, doesn't it make our arguments seem rather petty? Our pushing ourselves forward, our desires to have OUR point of view followed, our attempts to put other people down so that we can seem more important. In the next twenty-four hours watch yourself closely for those situations. Then think how Jesus might have behaved at those times.

RG

Colossians 3:15–17 (NIV)

Letting Christ 'permeate'

Let the peace of Christ rule in your hearts, since as members of one body you were called to peace. Let the word of Christ dwell in you richly as you teach and admonish one another with all wisdom, and as you sing psalms, hymns and spiritual songs with gratitude in your hearts to God. And whatever you do, whether in word or deed, do it all in the name of the Lord Jesus, giving thanks to God the Father through him.

Today's epistle offers three rules for the Christian life, which are relevant both corporately and individually. We are to 'let the peace of Christ *rule*' (v. 15)—the verb literally means to 'referee', to act as arbitrator. When disputes or strife comes, the decisive factor should not be who's right or wrong, or who's got more influence or power, but 'the peace of Christ'. We should let the peace of Christ arbitrate in our disputes and inner strife.

Then, we are to 'let the word of Christ dwell in us richly' (v. 16). It's an unusual phrase, and probably refers either to the Gospel (the saving message about Jesus) or to the actual teachings of Jesus, which the early Church studied and learnt by heart. Either way, the truth of Jesus is to 'dwell in you richly'—to soak into your deepest character, like sherry into a high-class trifle, as someone once put it to me! Christians are to be soaked in the attitudes and attributes of the Lord Jesus. We should let the word of Christ permeate.

Thirdly, whatever we do, 'in word or deed', we are to 'do it all in the name

of the Lord Jesus' (v. 17). Every time I see the sign on the DIY supermarket—'Do It All'—I think of this verse. In everything we attempt, the 'name' of Christ is to be involved. That means that even the routine things of daily life—the shopping, gardening, work, minding the children, driving the car—*all* are to be done 'in his name'. That doesn't mean, of course, that we are ostentatiously 'pious' about them, but that we recognize Christ's rule in every part of our lives.

Let the peace of Christ arbitrate. Let the word of Christ permeate. Let the name of Christ dominate. Lives infiltrated in this way at every level will be lives lived in peace, truth and usefulness.

A reflection

In what ways could I be more open to the peace and word of Christ? And in what parts of my life do I need to ensure that what I am doing—in word or deed—is 'in the name of Christ'?

DW

Mark 10:17–23 (NIV)

Top priority

A man ran up to [Jesus] and fell on his knees before him. 'Good teacher,' he asked, 'what must I do to inherit eternal life?' 'Why do you call me good?' Jesus answered. 'No-one is good—except God alone. You know the commandments: "Do not murder, do not commit adultery, do not steal, do not give false testimony, do not defraud, honour your father and mother."' 'Teacher,' he declared, 'all these I have kept since I was a boy.' Jesus looked at him and loved him. 'One thing you lack,' he said. 'Go, sell everything you have and give to the poor, and you will have treasure in heaven. Then come, follow me.' At this the man's face fell. He went away sad, because he had great wealth. Jesus... said... 'How hard it is for the rich to enter the kingdom of God!'

This is probably a familiar story for most readers. Before you go any further, read it again, and look for some point you have never noticed before.

As I did this, I became aware in a new way of the contrast between the man's enthusiasm at the beginning and his sadness at the end. He came running, expecting an easy answer to his question, 'How can I have eternal life?' All appeared well at first, as Jesus reminded him of all the commandments that he summarizes elsewhere: 'Love your neighbour as yourself' (Mark 12:31). 'Yes,' the man said eagerly, perhaps smugly; 'I've done all that.' But Jesus omitted the earlier commandments that he sums up with these words: 'Love the Lord your God with all your heart and with all your soul and with all your mind and with all your strength' (Mark 12:30). Love God first and foremost. That was

where the man had failed. It was not that his money and his possessions were bad things, but that they were at the centre of his life. That was why Jesus told him to shed them all, so that there could be room in his heart for God to take prime place. He did not want to make that choice, and he trudged away despondently.

What has prime place in your affections? Our possessions, family, home, leisure, work—even our Christian ministry—can easily usurp the Lord's rightful place in our lives.

A prayer

Lord Jesus, I find it easy to look disparagingly at this rich young man. But I ask you to show me what areas of my life have become too important and have displaced you.

RG

Mark 10:35–45 (NIV)

Me first!

James and John... came to him. 'Teacher, we want you to do for us whatever we ask...Let one of us sit at at your right hand and the other at your left in your glory.' 'You don't know what you are asking,' Jesus said... 'To sit at my right or left is not for me to grant. These places belong to those for whom they have been prepared.' When the ten heard about this, they became indignant... Jesus... said, '... those who are regarded as rulers of the Gentiles lord it over them... Not so with you. Instead, whoever wants to become great among you must be your servant, and whoever wants to be first must be slave of all. For even the Son of Man did not come to be served, but to serve, and to give his life as a ransom for many.

The disciples were slow learners. How discouraging it must have been for Jesus, especially as he neared the end of his time on earth! On Saturday we read of their argument about which of them was the greatest. Today we find the same atmosphere around, the same attitude of 'I'm best.' James and John no doubt felt discomfited at Jesus' rebuke; the others were angry with the brothers' presumption. But all of them were given a clear lesson about leadership. A truly great person has an inner core of confidence that does not need to worry about status, and is relaxed at the kitchen sink, on a platform speaking to 5,000 people or leading a committee full of strong-minded individuals. Christian leaders should be willing servants; humble without being 'Uriah Heep' creeps, yet confident without being bossy. Our supreme example is Christ himself.

'For even the Son of Man came not to be served, but to serve, and to give his life a ransom for many.' This is a verses that expresses the heart of the gospel. It is worth memorizing—plus its reference. And think about that word 'ransom;' 'sum demanded or paid for release of prisoner' (*Concise Oxford Dictionary*). Jesus' very life was the ransom paid to release us from being slaves to sin. Our response to his self-giving is to give ourselves to him in deep thankfulness.

A prayer

Lord, please forgive me when I look for importance. But thank you for giving your life to rescue me from my pride— among the rest of my sin.

RG

Mark 11:1–2, 7–11 (NIV)

Here comes the king!

As they approached Jerusalem and came to Bethphage and Bethany at the Mount of Olives, Jesus sent two of his disciples, saying to them, 'Go to the village ahead of you, and just as you enter it, you will find a colt tied there, which no-one has ever ridden. Untie it and bring it here... When they brought the colt to Jesus and threw their cloaks over it, he sat on it. Many people spread their cloaks on the road, while others spread branches they had cut in the fields. Those who went ahead shouted, 'Hosanna! Blessed is he who comes in the name of the Lord! Blessed is the coming kingdom of our father David! Hosanna in the highest!' Jesus entered Jerusalem and went to the temple. He looked around at everything, but since it was already late, he went out to Bethany with the Twelve.

Throughout his life Jesus showed that he was sure of his purpose; he knew where he was going, what his mission was. But never was this more marked than at the end of his life 'as he approached Jerusalem' and all the momentous events of the coming week.

His prior knowledge of the colt's availability is just one small detail that gives evidence of his awareness of what was to happen. Have you ever considered what might have been in Jesus' mind as he rode into the city on that first Palm Sunday? He deserved all the crowd's acclamations—and more. But those acclamations were hollow; a few days later the same people cried 'Crucify him!' I believe he knew already how fickle that crowd would prove. Their shouts and their branches are to be found in Psalm 118:26–27: 'Blessed is he who comes in the name

of the Lord... With boughs in hand, join in the festal procession...' Jesus knew the Scriptures well; and he knew that a few verses earlier 'The stone the builders rejected has become the capstone' (Psalm 118:22), a verse he quoted himself a few days later. He was that rejected stone, whose crucifixion and resurrection were to make him the cornerstone of the church. As he rode into Jerusalem, did he merely enjoy the applauding shouts? Or was there immense sorrow as he thought about what the week would bring?

Reflect

As God looks into our hearts, does he see a steadfastness of purpose like Jesus' own? Or does he see fickleness and wavering like that of the crowd?

RG

Mark 11:15–18 (NIV)

Righteous anger

Jesus entered the temple area and began driving out those who were buying and selling there. He overturned the tables of the money-changers and the benches of those selling doves... And as he taught them, he said, 'Is it not written: "My house will be called a house of prayer for all nations"? But you have made it "a den of robbers".' The chief priests and teachers of the law heard this and began looking for a way to kill him, for they feared him.

Jesus' last action before leaving Jerusalem the previous evening was to survey the scene in the temple courtyard. Passover was approaching, when people came to Jerusalem from the country for ceremonial cleansing; there was much activity round the temple, and plenty of opportunity for sharp practice. Jesus was dismayed by what he saw, but he did not react instantly; he returned to his friends' home in Bethany to think and pray overnight.

Next morning he knew what he had to do. He burned with righteous anger at the desecration of the holy place and at the way the gullible worshippers were being cheated. His actions and his plain words were another threat to the Pharisees' authority; after all, they had been conniving in the trading. They had long looked for a way to kill him; this was the last straw.

People nowadays sometimes use this incident as an excuse for their anger. They say, 'Jesus lost his temper; why shouldn't I?' Look closely at Jesus. When he showed his anger he did not lose control; his anger was over issues of holiness against his heavenly Father or injustice against the poor. But when the injustice was against him personally he did not retaliate. When he was in the dock and on the cross he deserved absolutely none of the slander and pain he received. Did he fight back? No, he 'entrusted himself to him who judges justly' (1 Peter 2:23). What an example to us when we are wronged! I have had big lessons to learn in this area of anger. There was a time in my life when my anger erupted against my children, my husband and my friends at any possible excuse. I needed to leave behind my attitude of 'Because I'm hurt I have a right to be angry' and to say instead 'Yes, I'm angry because I'm hurt; but I have no right to hang on to my anger or to use it as an excuse to hurt others.'

To think about

When they hurled their insults at him, he did not retaliate... instead he entrusted himself to him who judges justly.

1 Peter 2:23

RG

Mark 12:13–17 (NIV)

Pay what is due

They sent some of the Pharisees and Herodians to catch him in his words. They came to him and said, 'Teacher, we know you are a man of integrity. You aren't swayed by men, because you pay no attention to who they are; but you teach the way of God in accordance with the truth. Is it right to pay taxes to Caesar or not?...' But Jesus knew their hypocrisy. 'Why are you trying to trap me?' he asked. 'Bring me a denarius and let me look at it.' They brought the coin, and he asked them, 'Whose portrait is this? And whose inscription?' 'Caesar's,' they replied. Then Jesus said... 'Give to Caesar what is Caesar's and to God what is God's.' And they were amazed at him.

Different groups of Jesus' opponents sent representatives to trap him; in this case there was an unlikely alliance between the orthodox Jews and the secular Herodians. After their flattering approach the question appears innocent enough: 'Is it right to pay taxes to Caesar or not?' But the question was a minefield. If Jesus publicly advocated evasion of tax they could report him to the Romans and have him arrested as a revolutionary. But if he appeared to sell out to the hated Roman authorities he would lose his influence with the Jewish patriots whose cry was 'No tribute to the Romans!'

Jesus' reply incorporated some important New Testament principles about the individual and the state. The state is ordained by God, so that we live with order, not chaos; we cannot enjoy its benefits and opt out of its responsibilities. So 'give to Caesar what is Caesar's'—even though the coin showed not only the image of the emperor's face but also his claim to be divine. But 'God created man in his own image' (Genesis 1:27); people have God's image stamped on them. So 'give to God what is God's'. Our supreme loyalty should be shown in 100 per cent dedication to him.

For us, too, the question is not just about paying income tax—even though we are sometimes dismayed by the tax inspector's demands! As Christians we should be good citizens of the state to which we belong. But 'our citizenship is in heaven' (Philippians 3:20); we seek to live as obedient citizens of that eternal kingdom. If loyalties conflict, obedience to God must be supreme.

To reflect

In what ways should I be a better citizen of either the temporal or the eternal state?

RG

Mark 12:41–44 (NIV)

Give from your heart

Jesus sat down opposite the place where the offerings were put and watched the crowd putting their money into the temple treasury. Many rich people threw in large amounts. But a poor widow came and put in two very small copper coins, worth only a fraction of a penny. Calling his disciples to him, Jesus said, 'I tell you the truth, this poor widow has put more into the treasury than all the others. They all gave out of their wealth; but she, out of her poverty, put in everything—all she had to live on.

Yesterday we thought about taxes, the money that is required from citizens by the state. Today's verses are also about money changing hands; but they are not to do with demand and responsibility. They are about the generosity of a freewill offering, given from the heart to God. As Jesus watched the people who came to the temple worship putting their gifts into the box he did not judge their generosity by the amount. His insight looked past the loud clink of coins into their hearts. He knew that some gave out of their riches what they would not even notice; and he recognized the woman who gave her all out of her love for God.

It is often said that when God touches the heart he touches the pocket. A church's financial problems are often not rooted in the stringent circumstances of its members; the apparent financial problems are frequently spiritual problems at their root. For when a person's heart is open to God in love, the pocket—or the cheque book—is opened too. The one who has recognized God's generosity and has received from him finds it easy to hand over control of the bank balance, so that what is spent is under God's direction and what is given is given freely and joyfully. 'Each man should give what he has decided in his heart to give, for God loves a cheerful giver,' says St Paul (2 Corinthians 9:7). God's generosity is reflected in our own generosity of spirit—and of cash. What a contrast with the rich young ruler whom we met on Monday.

For our response

'Freely you have received, freely give' (Matthew 10:8). In what ways is God asking me to give to him, so that others may benefit?

RG

1 Corinthians 13:1–3 (NEB)

The best way of all

I may speak in tongues of men or of angels, but if I am without love, I am a sounding gong or a clanging symbol. I may have the gift of prophecy, and know every hidden truth; I may have faith strong enough to move mountains; but if I have no love, I am nothing. I may dole out all I possess, or even give my body to be burnt, but if I have no love, I am none the better.

Paul's famous passage on the nature of Christian love is usually read out of context. In fact, it comes in the midst of a discussion on the 'gifts of the spirit', especially speaking in tongues and prophecy.

The Corinthian Christians were proud of the variety of gifts that God had given them, though they placed too much emphasis on some at the expense of others. Paul wrote at length to correct their understanding. But, he said, there is one thing we must never lose sight of; that no gift has any meaning unless it is used in love. We may take our gift of tongues as a sign of the Spirit's presence in our lives. It is not. It is a gift that God has given, but the way it is used determines whether or not the Spirit is really at work in us. We may speak the very words of God to our church and society, but if they are not spoken in love, then whatever effect they have will be no sign of our spiritual state. And the same goes for other gifts, and even the greatest acts of self-sacrifice.

Of course, such self-denial often does spring from love. On the other hand, it can be a form of spiritual pride, a way of drawing attention to oneself. It is, says Paul, the motive that counts.

The important truth behind Paul's emphasis on love, is that our gifts, and even the success of our church or our ministry, in evangelism, pastoral care or whatever, is no indicator of our spiritual state. God gives gifts for the job we have to do, and he brings the work to fruition. At the same time, he seeks to work in our lives, to transform us into the image of Jesus. We must never mistake the one for the other. The true sign of a Spirit-filled life is love.

So today, in prayer and worship, seek for that genuine experience of God which overflows in love.

MM

Psalm 1:1–3 (NRSV)

Water works

Happy are those who do not follow the advice of the wicked,
or take the path that sinners tread,
or sit in the seat of scoffers:
but their delight is in the law of the Lord,
and on his law they meditate day and night.
They are like trees planted by streams of water,
which yield their fruit in its season, and their leaves do not wither.
In all that they do, they prosper.

A couple with their first garden bought a young tree from a garden centre. The nurseryman gave them two small bottles of liquid, one green, one red. 'Every morning,' he instructed them, 'give the tree a drop from the red bottle in two gallons of water; and every evening a drop from the green bottle in two gallons of water. I guarantee your tree will survive, or I'll give you your money back.' They followed his advice faithfully, and the tree flourished. What was in the bottles? Coloured ink! The secret, of course, was the water.

In the bare dusty mountains between Jerusalem and Jericho, I saw one or two dramatic streaks of brilliant green run down the rock, where a tiny watercourse still flowed even in summer. I was reminded of the request of Caleb's daughter, in Joshua 15, a text I made into a prayer during a 'desert' time of my life: 'Since you have given me land in the desert, give me also springs of water...' It only takes the merest trickle, even some underground dampness, for life to push its

way through. But for a fruitbearing tree, you need a river; and that is just what Jesus promised: 'Out of the believer's heart shall flow rivers of living water' (John 7:38).

It all depends, however, where you drink—or perhaps who you drink with (verse 1). The psalmist recommends drinking deep of God's wisdom, if we want to be fresh and fertile. The prosperity promised may not be material wealth, as the Israelites expected, and as some Christians expect even today. But it will be real, for 'I have appointed you to go and bear fruit, fruit that will last (John 15:16).

A way to pray

Jesus said to her, '...Those who drink of the water that I will give them will never be thirsty...' The woman said to him, 'Sir, give me this water.' Make her prayer your own. If you can, get a withered leaf and a fresh leaf to look at while you pray.

V.

Psalm 1:4–6 (NRSV)

Weeding

The wicked are not so, but are like chaff that the wind drives away.
Therefore the wicked will not stand in the judgment,
nor sinners in the congregation of the righteous,
for the Lord watches over the way of the righteous,
but the way of the wicked will perish.

'Big weed', says my 22-month-old son as we walk round our severely neglected garden. The weed is about four feet tall, much taller than John. Yet I pull it out easily from the drought-stricken ground. 'Little roots,' I explain, pointing to its flimsy base.

Old Testament people were much troubled by the lives of 'the wicked', the weeds who infested God's garden. Their theology told them that good people (those who obeyed God's moral and religious rules) would do well in life, and bad people (those who didn't) would suffer. But it didn't look that way. It bothered the author of Psalm 73: 'I saw the prosperity of the wicked... their bodies are sound and sleek... they are not plagued like other people... their eyes swell out with fatness...' Trying to understand the unfairness of life was 'a wearisome task'. Then he went into the temple to worship, and suddenly 'perceived their end... how they are destroyed in a moment... like a dream when one wakes'. Drawing near to God, one sees things from God's true perspective.

This is more than nodding sagely and saying 'Ah, but they'll come to a bad end'. What both psalms say is that those who are not rooted in God are rooted in nothing. Inevitably, when things get hot, they'll wither. In fact in terms of Psalm 1 the 'godless' are less than weeds, they are the husks winnowed from the grain and discarded— just windblown rubbish. The contrast between a well-rooted tree by a stream, and bits of useless fibre, could not be greater.

But telling the difference between wheat and weeds is not easy when they grow together in the same field (Matthew 13:24ff). Fortunately it is not our task, but God's, to do the weeding. Our responsibility may rather be to point out where the living water flows—so that everyone may choose to be a flourishing tree.

Reflect

'Those who are far from you will perish... but for me it is good to be near God... to tell of all your works' (Psalm 73:27–28). In what ways have you found it 'good to be near God'? Could you tell someone else about it? Pray for courage to do so.

VZ

Psalm 8:1–4 (Grail version)

Lost in space?

How great is your name, O Lord our God, through all the earth!
Your majesty is praised above the heavens;
on the lips of children and of babes you have found praise
to foil your enemy, to silence the foe and the rebel.
When I see the heavens, the work of your hands,
the moon and the stars which you arranged,
what are we that you should keep us in mind,
men and women that you care for us?

In London, light pollution from the street lamps is so great that we hardly ever see stars. But when my church went to a country house for a weekend away, we were overwhelmed by the thousands of points of light in the dark sky, each one a sun equivalent to our own; and beyond them, galaxy upon galaxy... And we think we have done well (and indeed we did) to reach our own little moon!

Contemplating the universe has a way of putting things into proportion. For the psalmist's audience, though their knowledge of the world was much smaller, the forces of nature were even greater than for us, since they were more mysterious and less controllable. In another respect too, their world was bigger—for they believed implicitly in a God who was greater than all the stars and worlds that God had made.

Make you feel small? Sometimes that can be a comfort; my fears and hopes which seemed so important recede into insignifance. Yet smallness can mean powerlessness too. That is where we discover the other side of the psalmist's God: the one who 'flung stars into space' is also the one who takes delight in the babbling of infants, just as their parents do. If so, he must listen to their crying too—and ours. 'But what am I?' said Tennyson, in his grief for a dead friend, 'An infant crying in the night, An infant crying for the light, And with no language but a cry.' This psalm assures us that the cry is heard.

A way to pray

Every night I pray out loud by my son's bedside. Once when he was about seventeen months he suddenly said one word: 'God'. I thought it was a pretty good start. If prayer is hard for you, find a place to sit in quiet and look at the world. Then just say that one word... and see what else comes.

V2

Psalm 8:5–9 (Grail version)

Acting managers

Yet you have made us little less than gods;
and crowned us with glory and honour,
gave us power over the works of your hands,
put all things under our feet.
All of them, sheep and cattle, yes, even the savage beasts,
birds of the air, and fish that make their way through the waters.
How great is your name, O Lord our God, through all the earth!

We ended yesterday with the image of an infant as powerless. But if my experience is anything to go by, the infant does not know she or he is powerless! My baby son learned within days that a mere cry from him could bring two large and powerful 'servants' running. And now he can use words, he relishes his power to make things happen just by making the right noises; and gets very frustrated when it doesn't work...

A large brain and an opposing thumb, plus the gift of language, have made us human beings the most powerful creatures on earth. 'The glory of God,' said the church father Irenaeus, 'is a human being fully alive.' But some would say the earth would be better off without us, as we use our power increasingly to destroy the planet we depend on.

The psalmist, in the face of hostile nature, saw human power as another demonstration of God's generosity: though we are so insignificant in the universe, yet God has given us the responsibility and the ability to order the world as we think best.

Perhaps the way we fulfil that task depends on how we see ourselves. If we view ourselves as powerless, we will let the world slide into ruin. If we think ourselves are God, we will exploit the world for our own gain and leave the consequences to the devil. Balance comes only in seeing ourselves from God's angle, as this psalm does: below the heavenly beings, above the animals, and standing before the face of God.

Ultimately it is over 'the works of your hands' that we are placed. If a great artist lent you their finest work for a short time, would you not feel extremely honoured and trusted? And would you not take infinite pains to keep it in good condition?

Consider

Man is neither angel nor beast; and the misfortune is that he who would act the angel acts the beast
Blaise Pascal

VZ

Psalm 19:1–4 (NRSV)

World view

The heavens are telling the glory of God; and the firmament proclaims his handiwork. Day to day pours forth speech, and night to night declares knowledge. There is no speech, nor are there words; their voice is not heard; yet their voice goes out through all the earth, and their words to the end of the world.

Some environmentalists accuse the Bible of being too human-centred. The concept of human 'dominion' over nature, they say, has led to uncaring exploitation of animals and the environment. Meanwhile Christianity is only interested in 'saving souls'.

This picture of the relationship between us and God could not be more different. Far from placing humanity at the centre, it portrays the depths of space 'telling the glory of God'—who to? Well, to each other: 'day to day... night to night'. They uttered their wordless song before there were people to hear it, and would still utter it if the human race destroyed itself. That God hears is enough.

For years I struggled with the idea of a creator God. I believed intellectually that God made the world, but I couldn't feel it. The God I met in most churches seemed much too small-minded to have made anything so complex, beautiful and lavish. Besides, many Christians seemed to care greatly about arguing that God made the world in six days, but apparently cared very little about what happened to it after that. 'If we were called as keepers to the evangelical zoo,' wrote poet Simon Jenkins, 'we would colour in the zebras and restrain the kangaroo... we'd paint a text on polar bears, I suppose John 3:16 would do'. We are sometimes considerably less imaginative than God!

It was only when I began to explore the biblical picture of God more fully that I started to relate to God as creator, who not only made the world, but is intimately involved with it, relishing its irrepressible life and variety. If our minds are expanded by the wonders of creation, we must let our image of God expand too.

Reflect

In Proverbs 8, Wisdom speaks: 'The Lord created me at the beginning of his work... when he marked out the foundations of the earth, then I was beside him like a master worker.. rejoicing before him always, rejoicing in his inhabited world, and delighting in the human race.' Do you rejoice in the created world? Can this itself be a form of prayer?

VZ

Psalm 19:7, 10, 12, 14 (NRSV)

The taste of truth

The law of the Lord is perfect, reviving the soul;
the decrees of the Lord are sure, making wise the simple...
More to be desired are they than gold, even much fine gold;
sweeter also than honey, and drippings of the honeycomb...
But who can detect their errors? Clear me from hidden faults...
Let the words of my mouth and the meditation of my heart
be acceptable to you, O Lord, my rock and my redeemer.

William Blake was a visionary, painter and poet. An art critic might concentrate on writing about his drawings and paintings; a literary critic would focus on his writings. But a biographer would move readily between one and the other, because their interest would be in Blake the man, who created both visual art and poetry.

So it is with this psalm. The jump from the stars and the sun to the laws of Yahweh, God of Israel, might seem sudden to us. But the psalmist's interest is in God the person, and all God does is relevant: both the creation which is given to everyone, and the special guidance God has given one chosen nation. So before verse 6 he uses the word 'God', and from verse 7 on 'the Lord', the special term for Israel's God. But it is the same God, the only God, who does both: creates and maintains the glorious sky, and gives wisdom and direction to human beings. So we move from the universal (the heavens) to the personal (the writer's desire for integrity) in a

seamless web, because the same God made and inhabits both.

The words for God's law pile up as though the writer loves it so much he wants to name it again and again: law, decrees, precepts, commandment, ordinances... in the end he can only compare it to the sweetest food he has ever eaten. Why such enthusiasm for a set of rules? Because the law is more: it is wisdom for all of life, the warp on which the weft of a good world is woven. If this is true of the Old Testament law, how much more is it true of the 'law of Christ', which is written on our hearts?

A way to pray

Choose one saying of Jesus which means a lot to you. Meditate on why you value it and what difference it makes to your life. Pray for the Spirit to help you obey it.

VZ

John 15:18–21 (JB)

Like master, like servant

If the world hates you, remember that it hated me before you. If you belonged to the world, the world would love you as its own; but because you do not belong to the world, because my choice withdrew you from the world, therefore the world hates you. Remember the words I said to you: a servant is not greater than his master. If they persecuted me, they will persecute you too; if they kept my word, they will keep yours as well. But it will be on my account that they will do all this, because they do not know the one who sent me.

I once knew someone who used to pray that the church in Britain would begin to suffer persecution. He wasn't a member of some anti-Christian cult, but a devout Christian. He believed, though, that the church could only attain real faith and power when it faced active opposition. I could never say 'Amen' to that prayer. Partly out of cowardice, and partly because I think he had the cause and effect the wrong way round.

Christians are called to bear witness to Jesus. Proclaiming the gospel always involves challenging the ways of the world. The gospel is a call to re-examine the way we live our lives, what we consider to be most important, to recognize our failings and sins, and to set up an alternate vision based on the teaching of Jesus and an encounter with the living God.

When that is done faithfully, there will indeed be opposition, for no one likes to be told they are wrong, and that goes double for those who hold power or benefit from the way things

are. Opposition and persecution are not the cause of effective witness, but the result of it.

In our country, and in much of the western world, we are more likely to encounter sneers and condescension than lions and stakes, though they can be smart quite enough for most of us. In other parts of the world, where the veneer of civilization and liberal attitude is thinner, violence and suffering can still be the reward for faithful discipleship.

Jesus met both forms of opposition, and today's reading is a reminder that no easy ride is promised his followers. We are called to walk in his footsteps, and the road is rough. But the destination is worth it, and on the way we have the best company of all: the presence of Jesus himself. So today, pray for the opportunity and the will to witness to him, and pray too for all those of the family of God who face the same consequences as he did.

MM

Psalm 29:1,3–4 (NRSV)

God in the storm

Ascribe to the Lord, O heavenly beings,
ascribe to the Lord glory and strength...
The voice of the Lord is over the waters;
The God of glory thunders, the Lord, over mighty waters.
The voice of the Lord is powerful; the voice of the Lord is full of majesty.

Some people are terrified of thunderstorms. They close the doors and windows and huddle in a corner. Myself, I love a good storm. After the oppressiveness of a sultry summer day, it clears the air and washes the whole world clean. There's something exhilarating about the flashes of lightning, the claps of thunder, and the rain which finally comes pouring.

For the psalmist, the power of a storm was evidence of the power of God, who created weather. As the storm hovers over the sea, he hears the distant thunder rolling and cannot help thinking of the one who created it. Ancient peoples all had a 'god of thunder', whether Jupiter or Thor, who sat on a cloud and hurled thunderbolts like spears. But this Hebrew picture is more than a fanciful image of the Thunderer. This is a God of whose glory the storm is just a pale reflection. The thunder is not his punishment of wayward humans, but a faint echo of his voice, which only has to speak and worlds are created: 'And God said, "Let there be light..."'

'Glory', 'strength', 'majesty'— these are words we don't encounter much in everyday life, where informality reigns and *Majesty* is just the title of a gossip magazine about 'royals'. Not many of us have encountered the awe-inspiring moment of approaching a monarch. The nearest I have come was when I used to worship in a very 'high' Anglican church with 'bells and smells', and on going up to the communion rail always felt I was kneeling at the feet of a King. To give the idea of 'glory' some content, you might go into a big Gothic cathedral, and feel how the soaring columns speak of a transcendent God. Or you might join the psalmist, and the next time a storm threatens, try facing it head on and using it to worship God.

A prayer

God of lightning and thunder, teach me what it means to fear you—and then to fear nothing else.

VZ

Psalm 29:5, 7–11 (NRSV)

Terror, triumph and trust

The voice of the Lord breaks the cedars; the Lord breaks the cedars of Lebanon... The voice of the Lord flashes forth flames of fire. The voice of the Lord shakes the wilderness...
The voice of the Lord causes the oaks to whirl,
and strips the forest bare; and in his temple all say, 'Glory!'.
The Lord sits enthroned over the flood; the Lord sits enthroned as king for ever. May the Lord give strength to his people!
May the Lord bless his people with peace!

In October 1987 the tail end of a hurricane swept over south-eastern Britain and destroyed trees, houses and vehicles over a huge area. I remember waking in the night to hear an unearthly wind, finding the electricity was off, thinking, 'They've dropped the bomb' and going back to sleep again! Later I saw the devastation wrought in precious woodlands, which would take years to restore.

In temperate Britain we rarely experience such events. But perhaps you have seen film of tornados, or of man-made explosions. Our reaction may be mixed: terror, yet a curious excitement at the power unleashed. We enjoy destruction—at a distance. As the psalmist watches the storm passing from the Mediterranean in the west, over the wooded hills of the north, and finally into Israel's eastern neighbour, his response is unmixed: a great shout of 'Glory!'.

But of course that shout comes from the congregation safe in the stone-built temple. What of the poor in shoddy housing or makeshift shacks, for whom hurricanes or floods make daily life precarious? Perhaps the last two verses are for them. Storms and floods bring danger, but God is still in charge, and it is from God that ultimate safety comes. Remember, however, that the prayer of verse 11 may be fulfilled by our building a world where the poor don't have to live in the hurricane zones.

Reflect

'Now there was a great wind... but the Lord was not in the wind... and after the wind an earthquake... but the Lord was not in the earthquake... and after the earthquake a fire... but the Lord was not in the fire... and after the fire a sound of sheer silence. When Elijah heard it, he wrapped his face in his mantle (1 Kings 19:11–13).' How have you heard God speak— overwhelmingly or 'in a still small voice'?

VZ

Psalm 104:1b, 2b, 3b, 5–6, 8–9 (NRSV)

Mostly harmless?

O Lord my God, you are very great... You stretch out the heavens like a tent... you make the clouds your chariot, you ride on the wings of the wind... You set the earth on its foundations so that it shall never be shaken. You cover it with the deep as with a garment; the waters stood above the mountains... They rose up to the mountains, ran down to the valleys to the place that you appointed for them. You set a boundary that they may not pass, so that they might not again cover the earth.

As I sat recently on a beach and watched the vast sea washing to and fro, I thought of that vision in Revelation, where the new heaven and earth appear, 'and there was no more sea'. I've always found that more of a threat than a promise. Growing up in the middle of Britain, as far from the coast as I could be, I learned to long for the sea: its might, its soothing rushing sound, its exhilarating smell.

But for the readers of this psalm, the 'Great Sea', the Mediterranean, was the source of all the dangers humankind faced. Sailors drowned in it, and from its depths came, in the legends, the huge sea-monster who represented the forces of chaos and destruction. 'In the beginning, the earth was a formless void, and darkness hovered over the face of the deep'... and one of God's first acts was to drive back the waters into 'their appointed place' and create dry land.

The opening of Psalm 104 is charged with a sense of God in control of all things. God is above nature, not subject to it as we are. The clouds and the wind, on which an agricultural people were so dependent, are merely God's transport. The earth is stable because God maintains it; the sea stays within bounds because God has confined it.

In Douglas Adams' *Hitchhiker's Guide to the Galaxy*, the entry for Earth reads 'Harmless'. A later edition expands this to 'Mostly harmless'. Yet we know that the earth holds all sorts of harm, both natural and man-made. In the psalmist's guide to the planet it is not harmless, but still 'under the best management'.

A prayer

Great God, who sustains the universe, show me that the things which frighten me—illness, loneliness, failure—are under your control too.

VZ

Psalm 104:14–30 (parts) (NRSV)

The circle of life

You cause the grass to grow for the cattle, and plants for people to use... wine to gladden the human heart, oil to make the face shine... The trees of the Lord are watered abundantly...
In them the birds build their nests... The high mountains are for the wild goats; the rocks are a refuge for the coneys...
The young lions roar for their prey... These all look to you to give them their food in due season; when you give it to them, they gather it up... when you hide your face, they are dismayed; when you take their breath away, they die...
When you send forth your spirit, they are created;
and you renew the face of the ground.

In the English National Gallery there is a famous painting of a forest fire by Piero di Cosimo. All the creatures of sky and earth flee the fire and show themselves to us: the birds, to quote Douglas Adams again, 'hang in the air the way that bricks don't'; the cattle and wild animals loom up as solid as houses. This psalm reminds me of that charming work of art, which like the psalm celebrates 'the circle of life'. Night and day, heights and valleys, birds and beasts and sea creatures, plenty and famine, birth and death: all are here and all are seen as under God's hand. Yet the writer is also realistic about the fact that God's provision is not automatic; both animals and people can go hungry and suffer.

A character in T.S. Eliot's *Sweeney Agonistes* muses that all there is is birth and copulation and death; that's all. Is that all? The psalm seems to suggest that the cycle of creation alone would be cause for praise. But it also shows us the God of creation who dwells both 'in a high and holy place' and 'with those who are.. humble in spirit' (Isaiah 57).

Julian of Norwich saw a vision of something round, as small as a hazelnut, in the palm of her hand, and God told her 'It is all that is made'. 'I marvelled', she said, 'that it could last, it was so small.' And she received the answer, 'It lasts, and ever shall last, because God loves it.'

Praise

O Lord, how manifold are your works!
In wisdom you have made them all;
the earth is full of your creatures.

Psalm 104:24

VZ

Psalm 148:1–6 (NRSV)

Hosanna in the highest

Praise the Lord! Praise the Lord from the heavens; praise him in the heights! Praise him, all his angels; praise him, all his host! Praise him, sun and moon; praise him, all you shining stars! Praise him, you highest heavens, and you waters above the heavens! Let them praise the name of the Lord, for he commanded and they were created. He established them for ever and ever; he fixed their bounds, which cannot be passed.

'Bless!' cried my toddler in the middle of Sunday service the other day. He was just repeating what he heard the worship leader say, and to him it was what you say when someone sneezes. But it sums up rather well the psalmist's response to the world: 'Bless!'

To ancient people there was no great divide between heaven and earth. The heavens, or sky, were full of spiritual beings, but also of created things: the sun, moon and stars, the 'waters above the heavens', which God had restrained from engulfing the earth. All these joined together in celebration of their own existence and of the God who had made them. You had only to look up to join in their celestial song of adoration.

When we look up in the sky today we see, perhaps, the tracks of jet planes, or at night the moon, which is now no longer unknown territory. We see space increasingly opened up by incredibly powerful telescopes, yet at the same time being filled with human rubbish dumped from space stations and satellites. But do we still see hosts of angels praising God, and hear the stars and planets joining the song? Even though we know now that space is not where God lives, yet still its vastness and its marvels may inspire in us a sense of wonder, a sense of a being so much greater than ourselves that even his least works are beyond our comprehension. 'Can you bind the chains of the Pleiades, or loose the cords of Orion?' God asked Job. And Job's answer was silent worship.

Consider

'When the sun rises,' said William Blake, 'do you not see a round disc of fire somewhat like a guinea? Oh no, no: I see an innumerable company of the heavenly host crying "Holy, holy, holy, is the Lord God Almighty"'.

VZ

Psalm 148:7–13 (NRSV)

Song of the earth

Praise the Lord from the earth, you sea monsters and all deeps,
fire and hail, snow and frost, stormy wind fulfilling his command!
Mountains and all hills, fruit trees and all cedars!
Wild animals and all cattle, creeping things and flying birds!
Kings of the earth and all peoples,
princes and all rulers of the earth!
Young men and women alike, old and young together!
Let them praise the name of the Lord,
for his name alone is exalted;
his glory is above earth and heaven.

Some modern thinkers see the earth as a self-regulating organism—the so-called 'Gaia hypothesis'. This psalm sees the earth as a God-praising organism, which exists neither for itself nor for humanity, but for its creator. From sea monsters through weather, landscape, plant life, animals of field and jungle and birds of the air, to women and men, all are united in offering a sacrifice of gratitude to the maker of all.

The other day I saw on television a production of Haydn's marvellous oratorio *Creation*. During the interval the presenter looked at the understanding of creation in biblical times, during Haydn's time, and today; his descriptions were accompanied by dramatic film of earth, sea and sky. The conclusion was that to believe in a 'Big Bang' rather than a six-day creation made no difference to our basic awe at the universe which inspired Haydn's music.

How the world was made is a matter of debate, often fierce. But for believers in the God that Israel believed in, there is no question about who is behind it all: the one who is to be praised in heaven and earth, the God and Father of Jesus Christ.

A way to pray

If you can get a copy of the Anglican Alternative Service Book, find the 'Benedicite' (page 90) and read it aloud as your prayer. Or write your own 'psalm' based on Psalm 104, calling on the creatures and things you see around you to praise God.

VZ

Proverbs 1:1–7 (NRSV)

True wisdom

The proverbs of Solomon son of David, king of Israel: For learning about wisdom and instruction, for understanding words of insight, for gaining instruction in wise dealing, righteousness, justice, and equity; to teach shrewdness to the simple, knowledge and prudence to the young—let the wise also hear and gain in learning, and the discerning acquire skill, to understand a proverb and a figure, the words of the wise and their riddles. The fear of the Lord is the beginning of knowledge; fools despise wisdom and instruction.

I wonder how Solomon the Wise is dealing with the news that his words of wisdom are to be commented on in 1997 by Adrian Plass. 'They should have asked a theologian,' he's probably complaining, 'or a trained moral philosopher, or *something*. The man is a rank amateur!' Well, hard cheese, Solly, old mate. You've been dead a long time, now it's my turn.

And that response of mine sums up, in a way, the attitude to wisdom in the nineties, doesn't it? Like food and travel and many other areas of our lives, so-called wisdom is packaged and labelled and made available, particularly on television, for independent selection by those who may well not be wise enough to do the selecting. In America recently we discovered with horror the lengths to which those 'audience participation' programmes will go to attract viewers.

'Do you suspect that your husband or wife is having an affair? If so, would you like to confront them with the evidence on national television without them having any previous warning?'

That's no exaggeration, and the morality of such broadcasting is justified by the argument that, in this instance, it will be helpful to other married couples who are facing problems. Thus, the ancient Romans might have claimed that the spectacle of Christians being eaten by lions was actually a practical examination of feline dietary problems.

Far from giving prudence to the simple, or instilling discipline where there is personal chaos, these events offer nothing but emotional creamcakes to viewers, some of whom are desperately in need of a sensible diet.

Prayer

Father, we know that the fear of the Lord does not sell many licences or much advertising but it remains the beginning of wisdom, and we pray that the young, the simple and the wise will find their counsel in you.

AP

Proverbs 1:20–23 (NRSV)

Spiritual thoughts

Wisdom cries out in the street... 'How long, O simple ones, will you love being simple? How long will scoffers delight in their scoffing and fools hate knowledge? Give heed to my reproof; I will pour out my thoughts to you; I will make my words known to you.'

This passage reminds me of my friend Rabbi Hugo Gryn, who was well known and greatly appreciated as a broadcaster. Sadly, Hugo died a few months ago. For four or five years Bridget and I met this master story-teller almost every week in the Maidstone studios of TVS to make a late-night 'God-slot' programme called 'Company'. This regional programme catered mainly for insomniacs, taxi-drivers, publicans, night-watchmen, and people who didn't manage to turn off the television quickly enough after the snooker finished, but it was fun to do, and we loved meeting people like Hugo.

In the course of many conversations we often discussed the differences, obvious and not so obvious, between Christianity and Judaism. One of the most interesting differences put forward by Hugo concerned knowledge and spirituality. In the Christian church, he suggested, knowledge is generally supposed to be acquired through the development of spirituality, whereas in the Jewish faith the more knowledge and understanding you have, the closer you are likely to come to a relationship with God.

I'm sure that these general tendencies are sometimes taken to extreme lengths by adherents to both faiths. Over a decade ago I was struck by the anger with which a small minority of those who attended charismatic churches rejected any suggestion that an intellectual approach to Christianity could have real worth. There seemed to be a fear that thinking and spirituality were in some way mutually exclusive, ridiculous though such a notion obviously is. Happily, the balance has now largely been restored in these areas, but I still encounter the odd person who tells me that it is 'dangerous to think'.

As for Hugo—the interesting thing is that his first real experience of God was an emotional one. Seventeen years old, and hiding in a corner of a German concentration camp one day, he wept for himself and the Jewish race and the whole world, and felt, for the first time, the reality and 'otherness' of God.

I feel so sad that Hugo can't be here to argue the point out a little further, but the opportunity may well come.

Prayer

Father, teach us to know
you and to love you. AP

Proverbs 1:29–31 (NRSV)

Criticism

Because they hated knowledge and did not choose the fear of the Lord, would have none of my counsel, and despised all my reproof, therefore they shall eat the fruit of their way and be sated with their own devices.

After reading this passage I asked myself how willing I really am to accept criticism or rebuke from man or God. On one level I can answer the question easily. I have always hated all criticism, especially the constructive variety, because you can't dismiss it scornfully. You have to do something about it!

Having said that, I am painfully aware of my need for helpful criticism, but it has to come from someone who provenly values me already. When my wife, Bridget, makes negative comments about something I've said or done or written I'm quite likely to get cross, but I will then take my crossness and her comments away into a corner for closer examination in private. More often than not I have to admit that she is absolutely right, and I do genuinely value her insights. I just wish that I did not have to go through this process of childish resentment each time, though.

On another level I think some things have changed. I now truly believe that we are qualified for God's service by our weaknesses rather than by our strengths (although my use of the word 'we' instead of 'I' might be significant).

Bridget and I worked for a time at Burrswood, the healing centre founded by Dorothy Kerin, who died in 1961, seven years before we joined the staff. One evening we were taken out to dinner by an elderly, very wise lady of Russian origin named Marina, who had been one of Dorothy Kerin's closest friends. During the meal Marina said something that I found very hard to take.

'Adrian,' she said, 'you are capable of great good and great evil. You are weak, but Bridget is strong.' Turning to Bridget, she said, 'You will have to protect him, my dear.'

This image of me as a sort of schizophrenic wimp didn't go down at all well at the time. I struggled desperately to maintain my hero image. In fact, although I don't think I showed it, I was furious. As the years have gone by, though, I have truly learned to value and appreciate that little nugget of wisdom. I carry it in a little side-pocket of my consciousness and take it out now and then when choices have to be made.

I still hate criticism, but I do thank God for it.

Prayer

Go on, say what you think—no, really, go on, say it. I don't mind...

AP

Proverbs 2:1–9 (NRSV)

Hidden treasure

My child, if you accept my words and treasure up my commandments within you, making your ear attentive to wisdom and inclining your heart to understanding; if you indeed cry out for insight, and raise your voice for understanding; if you seek it like silver, and search for it as for hidden treasures—then you will understand the fear of the Lord and find the knowledge of God. For the Lord gives wisdom; from his mouth come knowledge and understanding; he stores up sound wisdom for the upright; he is a shield to those who walk blamelessly, guarding the paths of justice and preserving the way of his faithful ones. Then you will understand righteousness and justice and equity, every good path.

The idea of hunting for understanding in the same way that one might hunt for hidden treasure is a fascinating one. Ever since I was a child I have dreamed of discovering something old and precious in a place that has been undisturbed for generations. Even now (my children are tired of hearing me say this), I fantasize about being left a very old house whose cellars and attics have remained untouched and unexplored for years. I find myself positively drooling over the prospect of hunting through dusty boxes and cupboards in the search for long-forgotten books and objects and pictures. Marvellous!

As this is never likely to happen, I shall content myself with the Bible, which is itself a storehouse of treasure, albeit one that is not always immediately visible or recognizable. Over the generations the sparkling gems of truth that lie between the covers of this remarkable book have tended to be obscured by the dust of over-familiarity, poor teaching, even poorer reading-out-loud, denominational bias and sheer fear of the vivid, non-religious life that it offers.

There are times, not continually, but frequently enough to bring me back to the search again and again, when some old dry-as-dust verse cracks open quite unexpectedly and there before me is the pure, precious metal of God's truth, often in the last place I thought to find it. When that happens I want to rush around waving my arms in the air like one of those old-timers in the westerns who've been panning for gold, and suddenly come across a shining reason to rejoice.

Prayer

Thank you for this treasure chest.
Guide us as we search its contents.

AP

Proverbs 2:12–22 (NRSV)

The prize

It will save you from the way of evil, from those who... rejoice in doing evil and delight in the perverseness of evil... You will be saved from the loose woman, from the adulteress with her smooth words, who forsakes the partner of her youth and forgets her sacred covenant; for her way leads down to death, and her paths to the shades; those who go to her never come back, nor do they regain the paths of life. Therefore walk in the way of the good... For the upright will abide in the land... and the treacherous will be rooted out of it.

I want to ask a question today that will probably annoy some of my brothers and sisters in Christ because they think the answer is such an obvious one. And anyway, they will probably add, it's not the sort of question you *should* ask. Here it is.

What's in it for us?

Vulgar, eh? But I have a feeling that a lot of Christians secretly want to ask that question, and I also believe that God wants us to be able to answer it, not just for ourselves, but also for people we meet who are outside the faith. Why should we want to be saved from the paths of wicked men? They seem to have quite a good time on the whole. And then there's the adulteress. Some of us might quite like to get involved with the adulteress or her male equivalent. It can't be *less* fun than Sung Eucharist at 8.00 a.m. on a wet Sunday morning, can it? Why should we be good? Why should we opt to be on the Lord's side?

What *is* in it for us?

Well, forget the right and proper answers for a moment and think about the kind of reply Jesus might have offered (not a bad guide for answering most questions). In yesterday's note we were talking about the hidden treasure to be discovered in the Bible. Jesus spoke about treasure as well. He said that we should store up treasure in heaven rather than on earth, and I'm sure he meant exactly what he said. He used the image of treasure very deliberately, and was clearly saying that, in heaven, the currency is different, but just as valuable. We shall be rich in the best possible way—the eternal way. That richness is manufactured from base metal of obedience and love, transmuted into the unfathomable joy of being with Jesus himself, a joy that is impossible to comprehend fully until we experience it in its fulness.

That's what's in it for us.

Prayer

Father, help us to keep our eyes on the true prize.

AP

Proverbs 3:1–8 (NRSV)

Health and wealth

My child, do not forget my teaching, but let your heart keep my commandments; for length of days and years of life and abundant welfare they will give you. Do not let loyalty and faithfulness forsake you; bind them round your neck, write them on the tablet of your heart... Do not be wise in your own eyes; fear the Lord, and turn away from evil. It will be a healing for your flesh and a refreshment for your body.

Well, this is interesting, isn't it? Read verse 2 again and you might see what I mean. The writer appears to be saying quite clearly that conscientious application of his teaching and commandments will result in a long life and material gain.

When we were touring Australia last year we found a growing interest in and adherence to what is commonly named the 'health and prosperity' movement. Those who embrace such teaching believe, as I'm sure you already know, that if Christians make the kingdom of God a priority in their lives, God will be more or less obliged to bless them with material wealth and physical good health. I presume that verses like the one just quoted would be used by followers of this doctrine to support their claims.

So, perhaps they're right. The Old Testament's full of people getting rich when God's pleased with them. What do you think? After all, there it is in black and white—many years and prosperity. Let's go for it!

Actually, I'm *not* going for it, if you don't mind. There are very serious problems with using the Old Testament as a source of doctrine unless it is read and considered in the light of what Jesus teaches us through the Gospels. Without going into too much detail, I'd just like us to imagine how Jesus would react on being informed that his followers feel pretty confident that they are entitled to a reasonable income and substantial health benefits. This man who said that we would suffer just as he had, only more so; who sent out his followers without so much as a pair of sandals; who said that the poor are blessed; who sorrowed over the problems rich people would have in entering the kingdom of heaven; how would he have reacted?

I'll tell you how I think he would have reacted. I think he would have laughed until he cried. Or, come to think of it, he might have just cried.

Prayer

Lord, how long will it be before your people know what being rich and healthy really means?

AP

Proverbs 3:11–14 (NRSV)

Discipline

My child, do not despise the Lord's discipline or be weary of his reproof, for the Lord reproves the one he loves, as a father the son in whom he delights. Happy are those who find wisdom, and those who get understanding, for her income is better than silver, and her revenue better than gold.

A friend of mine was telling me about his divorce as we drove back from the north of England.

'We were married for a very long time,' he said, 'and hardly anyone knew there were problems in our relationship. When it reached the stage where divorce was looking like the only real option, my wife and I decided to send out a letter to quite a large number of people—close friends, of course, relatives, and some of the people at our church. It was easier than having to explain it a hundred times over.'

I nodded. 'And did they all write back?'

'Oh, yes, we had some wonderful replies—a lot of understanding and compassion. People were really warm in the way they responded.'

'Were there any replies you didn't like?'

'There was one,' he replied thoughtfully, 'I don't mean it was unpleasant. It wasn't. It was very friendly. The person who wrote it said that he was sure we were doing the right thing.'

'What's wrong with that?'

He tilted his head and sucked air through his teeth. 'I dunno, I suppose it was just that the person concerned didn't actually know me all that well, and he'd hardly ever met my wife, so it seemed a little bit—well, a bit unhelpful to sound so sure that divorce was the right way to go. By contrast,' he went on, 'the two replies I valued most were just as warm and supportive, but they included a firm but gentle question about whether there could be an alternative to divorce. In effect, they were asking if we'd properly thought and prayed through the issue before making such a serious decision. I really appreciated those two letters.'

PRAYER

Father, thank you for the times when our friends show real godly love by not letting us easily get away with things that could be bad for us, as well as supporting us with compassion and warmth. Help us not to reject your discipline, given directly or through someone else, when that's exactly what we need.

AP

Proverbs 3:19–21 (NRSV)

Fear

My child... keep sound wisdom and prudence, and they will be life for your soul and adornment for your neck... your foot will not stumble. If you sit down, you will not be afraid; when you lie down, your sleep will be sweet. Do not be afraid of sudden panic, or of the storm that strikes the wicked; for the Lord will be your confidence.

Here are some questions relating to this passage. Don't worry—I'm not putting these down to make you feel bad about yourself. I'm going to try to face up to my own answers. If your response is the same as I think mine is going to be, then we'll pray together. If it's not, you can pray for me and those like me.

When I sit down, am I afraid?

The answer to that question is 'Yes, I *am* afraid.' There is a gloom that has shadowed my heart since I was a very young child. This shadow was cast by difficult events that I had no control over during that period, and also by some very injudicious reading of frightening books as I moved towards my teens. I would dearly like to be free of that shadow.

When I lie down, is my sleep sweet?

Generally speaking, no, it is not sweet. I ought to say immediately that one substantial reason for this is my weight (too great), and my evening meal (too much and too late). Those aren't the only reasons, though. Sleep is still a fearful land for me, a place where you would be unwise to let yourself relax completely. I used to suffer from something called Sleep Paralysis, which didn't help. It comes

back sometimes when I'm very tense. I would love to enjoy sweet sleep.

Do I have no fear of sudden disaster or of the ruin that overtakes the wicked?

This question is not so easy to answer. That same shadow of gloom I have already mentioned is sometimes inhabited by phantoms of inevitable doom and destruction at the worst possible times, but I have much greater confidence nowadays that I cannot be overtaken by the consequences of my sin. God loves me, and because of Jesus I am saved. I don't think I've ever written it as bluntly before. Perhaps I believe it more bluntly.

That still leaves the problems with night-time and shadows and sleep. Let's pray about them.

PRAYER

Father, I know I'm not the only one who finds the nights difficult. Grant us judgment and discernment in dealing with the practical things that need changing, and give us your peace and wisdom to wear like ornaments around our necks at the moment when the shadows begin to fall.

AP

Proverbs 4:7–8 (NRSV)

Get wisdom

The beginning of wisdom is this: Get wisdom, and whatever else you get, get insight. Prize her highly, and she will exalt you; she will honour you if you embrace her.

Do you remember an item of news some years ago about a young couple who auctioned off everything they owned, including their house and furniture, in order to raise money for starving refugees in a distant country? I was quite young at the time, probably around sixteen, and I had only just become a Christian. I wasn't at all sure what to think about this extravagant gesture (we found out what we thought about things by asking the clergy usually), but I think I veered from admiration of such a generous, wholehearted act of giving, to concern that the young couple concerned were not exercising their stewardship properly (stewardship was a term I'd heard of for the first time only recently). Another part of me, pre-Christian and probably saner than the parts of me that had produced the first two responses, thought there was something very silly about ending up with nothing and having to rely on others to give you the things that you couldn't have because you'd just given them away to someone else. Or something like that.

Could this be the kind of wildly expansive act that the writer of the above passage is talking about when he says that we should acquire understanding, whatever the cost? Is there really a way in which we can exchange riches of some kind for the supreme gift of wisdom? I suspect that there is a way, but I am absolutely sure that the cost is much greater than the loss of material belongings or the contents of a bank account.

The clue lies in the readiness with which Jesus' disciples followed him when they were called. It was a readiness, not just to physically follow him, but to place him at the very top of their individual lists of what was most important to them. In dropping their own rights to decision and destiny those men gained the reality of his wisdom and power in their lives, despite the fact that there was no magical transformation of their personalities at that time. It can still happen today, but I don't think it happens much.

Prayer

Father, show us individually what it means to put Jesus first in our lives. We can't actually follow him physically through Luton or Carlisle in 1997. How should we do it?

AP

Proverbs 4:20–24 (NRSV)

Keep your heart

My child, be attentive to my words; incline your ear to my sayings. Do not let them escape from your sight; keep them within your heart. For they are life to those who find them, and healing to all their flesh.
Keep your heart with all vigilance, for from it flow the springs of life.
Put away from you crooked speech, and put devious talk far from you.

This injunction to 'keep your heart... for from it flow the springs of life' offers a deceptively simple challenge and a warning that is quite alarming. The challenge is to look clearly at what is in my heart, and the warning is that whatever my heart contains will be apparent in my life through actions or words.

Kinda makes you wanna sit tight an' say nuthin', don' it?

Those of us who have mapped the geography of our selves know what a dispiriting exercise this can be. We start off okay, marching boldly towards the edge of our talent or our goodwill or our patience or our generosity, and are suddenly brought up short by a precipice, usually at a point where it seemed as if the firm ground might go on for ever. Setting off in a different direction we discover that exactly the same thing happens. In fact, it happens again and again and again, until we start learning the shape and limits of what we are. For some this is a very welcome piece of learning—settle down and get on with it, they would say. For others, those with the blood of explorers in their veins, it is a kind of prison.

This is how many of us feel about the contents of our hearts. We look for enough compassion to care truly about the world and find a pathetically limited ability to place our arms around the suffering of others. We search for the strength of will and forgiveness to set ourselves and those we hate free from chains of resentment and bitterness, only to find weakness and a cherishing of hurts. We hunt within our hearts for the courage to fight when everything in us wants to lie down, and to wait quietly when we want to fight, but discover instead a self-indulgence that *will have* what it is greedy for.

We stand on the shore of our own lives, calling out to God that we can go no farther unless he provides a way.

PRAYER

Father, we know that we are weak and limited and that our hearts are not clean, but Jesus told us that he is The Way by which we shall find life and power. We ask that he should inhabit the throne of our hearts and live his righteousness through us.

AP

Proverbs 5:15–20 (NRSV)

Sex

Drink water from your own cistern, flowing water from your own well… Let your fountain be blessed, and rejoice in the wife of your youth, a lovely deer, a graceful doe. May her breasts satisfy you at all times; may you be intoxicated always by her love. Why should you be intoxicated, my son, by another woman and embrace the bosom of an adulteress?

A young man called Steve said to me, 'Is it normal to fancy other women after you're married?' He was one of those clear-eyed individuals who spend the first part of their lives expecting, and generally speaking discovering, that life is a good, wholesome, rewarding sort of affair. He and his wife, Samantha, had fallen head-over-heels in love when they were twenty, and enjoyed a fairy-tale wedding. Now she was pregnant, and Steve was dismayed to find his young wife's hugely inflated body not attracting him as it had done. Indeed, his eyes were straying lustfully in the direction of other, slimmer females who were—well, not Samantha.

For Steve, this was a shadow over his life, a profound failure in his relationship with Sam and with God. He felt somehow mucky and diminished by the experiences he was having.

'I keep thinking,' said Steve, 'about Jesus saying that if you just *look* at another woman with desire you're already committing adultery. That means I've already committed adultery fifteen times since I got up today.'

I think my friend might have been a little taken aback by the matter-of-fact way I responded to his problem.

'Consider these points, Steve,' I said. 'One, there may be some men who haven't fancied other women after getting married, but if you got them all together they'd fit quite easily into a large wardrobe.

'Two, Jesus wasn't silly or unrealistic. He knew what human beings are like. He was one. He never compromised the truth, but he knew all about temptation, and he's more interested in helping you deal with that, than organizing thunderbolts because you're fantasizing about Bessie next door.

'Third, sex is a crucial part of being married, but real love is a complex, maturing thing. It takes a lot of time and work, but you can end up with something rich and right and priceless. The sex'll get sorted out, you'll see. Don't give up before you've started, mate. The best is yet to come.'

Prayer

Father, marriages are falling apart all around us. Help us to be strong and wise in our relationships, and to depend on you like children. AP

Proverbs 8:1–11 (NRSV)

Better than gold

Does not wisdom call, and does not understanding raise her voice? On the heights, beside the way, at the crossroads she takes her stand; beside the gates in front of the town, at the entrance of the portals she cries out: 'To you, O people, I call, and my cry is to all that live. O simple ones, learn prudence; acquire intelligence, you who lack it... Take my instruction instead of silver, and knowledge rather than choice gold; for wisdom is better than jewels, and all that you may desire cannot compare with her.

Why *don't* people choose wisdom instead of silver or gold? Why are the very things that attract us to other people, whether they be kindness, gentleness or quiet wisdom, the last things we want for ourselves? Strange, isn't it?

I have seen this phenomenon very clearly in the lives of my own children as they've grown up. They have always loved and instinctively wanted to be close to people who had the qualities I've just described, but, certainly through their teenage years, for themselves they wanted something tougher and more brassily impressive to show off than these unselfish talents. I suppose most children pass through this phase, but some of us never come out the other side.

Take me, for instance. Even now, when I'm forty-eight, and ought to know better, I occasionally find myself carefully setting out to impress another person with some pathetic achievement or other. Almost invariably this other person will be one of these truly nice people who really, really do seem

to want to hear me mouthing off vainly about myself. Even as I speak, I find myself looking at the person opposite and wishing that he or she could see in me the qualities of receptivity and kindness that I see in them.

When this happens I get quite disturbed, and I pray sincerely to God that I will eventually lose my obsession with myself and the way in which the rest of the world sees me. In the end, I would like to be so genuinely interested in other people that their image of me doesn't concern me any more.

An interesting thought occurs to me. *If* this miraculous change ever occurs—I won't know it's happened, will I? So, perhaps it's happened! No, I don't think so either...

PRAYER

Father, lots of us want the applause without the rehearsal. Help us to value the qualities that are truly attractive and to keep our mouths shut until we gain some of them.　　AP

Proverbs 8:22–26 (NRSV)

Wise notes

The Lord created me at the beginning of his work, the first of his acts of long ago. Ages ago I was set up, at the first, before the beginning of the earth. When there were no depths I was brought forth, when there were no springs abounding with water. Before the mountains had been shaped, before the hills, I was brought forth—when he had not yet made earth and fields, or the world's first bits of soil.

Wisdom is a recurring tune in the symphony of creation, running on for ever, whatever else fails.

Have you ever written any music? Until about ten years ago I had never even thought about writing serious songs. Working in a succession of residential establishments we did have a go at putting together lyrics for songs to be performed in pantomimes and revues, but we always relied on the nearest keyboard wizard to supply the actual music.

Then, during a period of enforced idleness, as I was just beginning to find out how invigorating it could be to tell the truth, I suddenly wanted to write songs more than anything else. I felt terribly frustrated because I didn't know how to do it. I had an old guitar that I swear tried to hide in corners when it saw me coming, but I was somewhat limited by the fact that I could only play three chords with any confidence. The dull, throbbing, strumming noise that I produced with my right hand was equally uninspiring, and I was beginning to feel a bit discouraged when a friend suggested that I should just write the words and the tune of each song and then he'd 'turn them into music'.

The joy of it!

I shall never forget the first occasion that he turned up with a tape and put it on my cassette player. MY TUNE came out of those speakers sounding so splendid that I hardly recognized it. It was sung by someone who could really sing, and it was accompanied by drums and guitars and a keyboard and goodness knows what else. My little tune had been turned into music!

It was a small parable, applying not just to my miserably unproductive life at that time, but to the lives of many people who feel it's hardly worth offering God the unsophisticated melody of time, effort or talent that they possess.

My advice is—offer it! You'll be amazed what an expert can do with a simple tune.

PRAYER

*Father, make beautiful music
with our lives.*

AP

Proverbs 8:27–31 (NRSV)

Being there

When he established the heavens, I was there, when he drew a circle on the face of the deep, when he made firm the skies above... when he assigned to the sea its limit... when he marked out the foundations of the earth, then I was beside him, like a master worker; and I was daily his delight, rejoicing before him always, rejoicing in his inhabited world and delighting in the human race.

I feel rather jealous of Wisdom in this passage, don't you? Fancy having been there! Just imagine being present when God was drawing up the blueprints for Creation at the beginning of time, and watching as those plans were carried out on such an awe-inspiring scale. Nothing that Hollywood has ever produced comes close to the reality of what happened then. I love the thought of Wisdom being filled with delight as each day brought yet another amazing spectacle. In fact, I feel very sad that I won't ever see it, and this brings me to a little private fantasy that I'd like to share with you.

I've arrived in heaven, right? Some kind of conference-centre-managing-type angel has shown me to my mansion, no doubt situated right next door to someone I was sure would never make it, and I'm just flicking through the Heaven brochures before taking a stroll around. I learn to my surprise that there's a video shop just up the golden street, and I decide to pay it an immediate visit. When I get there I discover to my unutterable joy that the videos on offer cover every period of history from the beginning of time to the moment when I shuffled off my own particular mortal coil.

Incredible prospect, eh? Just think—on my heavenly Friday nights I can take out 'The Battle of Waterloo' and 'The Invention of the Wheel', or I might decide to settle down and watch 'Henry the Eighth'. Or perhaps I'd decide to get out a tape called 'The Jurassic Era', and enjoy footage of dinosaurs that would make Speilberg's efforts look pale by comparison. I might get a few friends together and spend the whole of one week watching 'Genesis', followed on Sunday by 'Exodus', starring the real Moses, who will almost certainly look nothing like Charlton Heston. Come to think of it, I could get Moses to come over and watch it with me—fill me in on all the details. Yes, that's what I'll do...

Prayer

Father, forgive my silliness, but I would love us all to warm up to the idea of heaven, and particularly to the idea of experiencing the joy described in this passage, simply because we are in your presence.   AP

Proverbs 9:10–12 (NRSV)

Beginnings

The fear of the Lord is the beginning of wisdom, and the knowledge of the Holy One is insight. For by me your days will be multiplied, and years will be added to your life. If you are wise, you are wise for yourself; if you scoff, you alone will bear it.

I wish I could remember who said this and that about various things. I sound like P.G. Wodehouse on a bad day, don't I? I've been trying to recall who said something like, 'Give me the child for the first seven years of his life, and I will give you the man.' I think it might have been the Jesuits, but, there again, it might not.

Whoever did say it was right. During the years when I worked with children in trouble of various kinds, I saw, again and again, how experiences of early childhood produced patterns and attitudes that were probably there for life. Some teenagers were fighting an intense and essential battle to replace longstanding, negative ideas about themselves with more balanced and practically useful self-images.

Raymond, for instance, had already come through the trauma of his mother's divorce, and was subsequently rejected by his mother and her new husband for reasons that had more to do with making their own nest more cosy than anything Raymond had done. I remember playing snooker with Ray after he heard that he would not be going home, and listening as he poured out the feelings of guilt and failure that he had lived with all his life.

Raymond blamed himself for *everything*, and is probably spending the rest of his life dealing with that very damaging illusion.

What does all this have to do with the passage? Well, I think it might be worth reflecting, as we read these familiar words about the fear of the Lord being the beginning of wisdom, that some Christians have had an equally unfortunate journey through the early years of their adoption into the family of God. Because of such problems as poor teaching, over-heavy pastoring, unfortunate encounters with enthusiastic but wrong people and various other difficulties, a lot of the believers that I meet have a very low opinion of themselves (not the same thing as humility), and need a lot of help in regaining a balanced view of their worth in the eyes of God. Let's pray for them.

Prayer

Father, some of your children have had very unfortunate spiritual childhoods because of the mistakes of others. Help them to understand that you see them as they really are, and that, after a new beginning, they will find wisdom of their own.　　AP

Genesis 6:1–8 (NRSV)

Days of legend

When people began to multiply on the face of the ground, and daughters were born to them, the sons of God saw that they were fair; and they took wives for themselves of all that they chose. Then the Lord said, 'My spirit shall not abide in mortals for ever, for they are flesh; their days shall be one hundred and twenty years.' The Nephilim were on the earth in those days—and also afterward—when the sons of God went in to the daughters of humans, who bore children to them. These were the heroes that were of old, warriors of renown. The Lord saw that the wickedness of humankind was great in the earth... And the Lord was sorry that he had made humankind on the earth, and it grieved him to his heart. So the Lord said, 'I will blot out from the earth the human beings I have created—people together with animals and creeping things and birds of the air, for I am sorry that I have made them.' But Noah found favour in the sight of the Lord.

The first four verses of Genesis 6 must be among the most mysterious in the Old Testament. The writer takes a common theme from pagan myth and legend; that of the gods who take human wives. The resulting offspring are the mighty Nephilim (a name whose meaning is unclear), legendary warriors of the ancient times.

Unlike that in pagan legends, however, this unnatural union between supernatural beings and human women is seen as abhorrent. The result is not a race of demigods, but God's reducing of human lifespan, which up to now has been measured in hundreds of years. This legendary incident is seen as yet another example of the theme of the first part of Genesis—the attempt by humans to deny their origins as God's creatures, and aspire to divinity on their own terms. The breakdown of the division between the orders of creation is one symptom of the corruption that has spread throughout humankind.

We often hear the complaint that God 'ought to do something' about the terrible things that happen in the world. Here he does. But the plan fails. God cannot wipe out everyone, for there is at least one man who does not deserve to die: Noah.

And that is the ultimate problem. God may wipe out all but one. Yet that one is still human, prone to sin, and in need of redemption. So the point of the story is foreshadowed at the start. Destruction is not the way that God really works. If he is going to 'do something', it will not be that.

MM

Genesis 6:9–15 (NRSV)

The righteous man

These are the descendants of Noah. Noah was a righteous man, blameless in his generation; Noah walked with God. And Noah had three sons, Shem, Ham and Japheth. Now the earth was corrupt in God's sight, and the earth was filled with violence. And God saw that the earth was corrupt; for all flesh had corrupted its ways upon the earth. And God said to Noah, 'I have determined to make an end of all flesh, for the earth is filled with violence because of them; now I am going to destroy them along with the earth. Make yourself an ark of cypress wood; make rooms in the ark, and cover it inside and out with pitch. This is how you are to make it: the length of the ark three hundred cubits, its width fifty cubits, and its height thirty cubits.'

Noah was saved, we are told, because he was 'righteous and blameless'. Yet this does not mean he was perfect and sinless. 'Righteous' is a term which the Bible uses to describe someone who keeps God's laws, which include rules about how to behave when one sins. It is not sinlessness which saves Noah, but the fact that he 'walked with God'.

Of all the people in the earth, Noah has not forgotten about God. He still knows his creator, and seeks his company. It is this which makes Noah 'deserving' of salvation.

Read in this light, the story echoes another important theme of both Genesis and the whole Bible. The source of true life is found in God alone, and to ignore him can result only in destruction.

We need not fear the heavens opening in response to our abandonment of God. Yet without him, the message remains the same. Life lived only for self, and only by human effort and values is life which is doomed to perish. Eternal life, and the depth of life for which we were created, is found only by walking, however imperfectly, with God.

God's response, then, to Noah's righteousness is to provide him with an escape. Note that the ark is designed by God, not Noah. Noah's job is simply to build it. Salvation always comes from God. Our part is to respond to it in faith and obedience, another term for 'walking with God'.

Pray

Father, keep us by your side, so that we can find the true nature of life.

MM

Blueprints

'Make a roof for the ark, and finish it to a cubit above; and put the door of the ark in its side; make it with lower, second and third decks. For my part, I am going to bring a flood of waters on the earth... everything that is on the earth shall die. But I will establish my covenant with you; and you shall come into the ark, you, your sons, your wife and your sons' wives with you. And of every living thing, of all flesh, you shall bring two of every kind into the ark, to keep them alive with you; they shall be male and female... Also take with you every kind of food that is eaten, and store it up; and it shall serve as food for you and for them.' Noah did this; he did all that God commanded him.

The writer does his best to make the details of the story realistic. The size of the ark is immense; it is divided into three decks of rooms. There is a food supply and a breeding pair of every animal from snails to snakes and from elephants to... you get the picture.

Then the chapter ends with a simple statement; 'Noah did this.' Can you imagine the amount of effort involved? Not just the building, which would have taken years, not even the gathering of forty days' worth of food for the biggest zoo in history, but the collection of animals?

Perhaps we're not meant to dwell too much on the details. But then again, perhaps we are. God has provided Noah with the blueprint of the ark; indeed, with the pattern for his salvation. But Noah has to put it all together. No doubt we can imagine God helping—the animals arriving two by two when needed. Even so, it was a pretty stupendous task.

There again, that is the way God works. He provides the way of salvation, but that salvation is put into practice by his people. God provides Jesus, and the gospel call to faith, but it is up to us to respond, and to put it into practice. There are obstacles and setbacks. There are times when the task seems insuperable, the temptation to turn aside irresistible. Were there days when Noah went to bed muttering that it would be easier to take swimming lessons? At the end, though, the job is done, and God is shown to be right. He doesn't set an easy task, but he always sets a necessary one.

Pray

Father, give us grace to persevere with you when the going is difficult. Help us to remember that the work we do, the life we live, is part of your plan of salvation.

MM

Genesis 7:11–16 (NRSV)

Seeking refuge

The windows of the heavens were opened. The rain fell on the earth forty days and forty nights. On the very same day Noah with his sons... and Noah's wife and the three wives of his sons entered the ark, they and every wild animal of every kind, and all domestic animals of every kind, and every creeping thing... every bird, every winged creature. They went into the ark with Noah, two and two of all flesh in which there was the breath of life. And those that entered, male and female of all flesh, went in as God had commanded him; and the Lord shut him in.

In the beginning, when God created the heavens and the earth, so the opening chapter of Genesis tells us, he separated the waters of the great deep of chaos, and placed the earth like a bubble between them. Now chaos returns and the waters of the deep crash back to reclaim the fragile island of creation.

It's a mythic picture of the results of sin. Those who have abandoned God find that all which ultimately remains is chaos and destruction. But for the few who have stuck with their creator there is safety and a place of refuge. God himself closes the door that shuts out the forces of destruction.

The powerful image of the ark has struck a chord with many writers. It is behind Matthew's picture of the disciples finding safety from the storm in a boat with Jesus (Matthew 14:32). Peter likens baptism to rescue from the waters of chaos into the ark of the people of God (1 Peter 3:20f).

Nowadays many Christians are uncomfortable with the image of God or the church as a refuge. It is seen as admitting the charge that religion is escapism or a crutch for those who cannot cope with the world. There are several answers to that. I for one do not mind admitting that I can't cope alone, and that God gives me strength and hope. The world, as it is, is well worth escaping from, at least for a time.

And that is the second point. Noah is safe from the flood, but he will emerge to start the world again. Christians find refuge in God and his worship, but they emerge strengthened to serve him in the world.

Finally, the escape is not just from the pressures of the world, but from a life lived without God, which is, in the end, no life at all.

Pray

Father, thank you for your salvation, your refuge from futility, and the hope you give.

MM

Genesis 8:6–12 (NRSV)

Seeking signs

At the end of forty days Noah opened the window of the ark... and sent out the raven; and it went to and fro until the waters were dried up from the earth. Then he sent out the dove from him, to see if the waters had subsided... but the dove found no place to set its foot, and it returned to him to the ark... So he put out his hand and took it and brought it into the ark with him. He waited another seven days, and again he sent out the dove from the ark; and the dove came back to him in the evening, and there in its beak was a freshly plucked olive leaf; so Noah knew that the waters had subsided... Then he waited another seven days, and sent out the dove; and it did not return to him any more.

After nearly a year, the tops of the mountains are again visible, and the world seems to be returning to normal. Noah has had a long wait, and is now eager for some sign that all is well. Eventually it comes, but it is no miracle, nor even the voice of God that Noah has come to know so well.

Instead, he must send out birds to seek for dry land, and deduce the state of affairs from the way they behave. In fact, throughout the story there is a sense of realism that balances the mythic quality. God saves, but not by waving a magic wand. Noah is kept safe, but not in some enchanted fairy land. Instead, he must work with the material to hand, constructing the ark, pitching on the waters, landing on a mountain range, and seeking reassurance in his own way.

It is a characteristic of almost all the biblical literature that God is seen working through the things of the world, and not against their nature.

Even miracles are not cure-alls. The dead, like Lazarus, may be raised, but then their life goes on. Noah is saved from the flood, but he must raise crops and carry on his life.

The reason for this attitude is the biblical doctrine of creation. God made the world, and so it is the proper place, with the proper opportunities, to know and serve him. The 'spiritual', 'divine' aspects of life are not a separate compartment divided from the rest of reality. God's will is made known as readily by the flight of a dove as by the words of a prophet, or as much by the everyday circumstances of our lives as by an exalted experience of prayer or worship.

Pray

Father, give me eyes to see and ears to hear what you are doing in the world, and what your will is for me.

MM

Genesis 8:15–22 (NRSV)

Never again

Then God said to Noah, 'Go out of the ark, you and your wife, and your sons and your sons' wives with you. Bring out with you every living thing that is with you of all flesh—birds and animals and every creeping thing that creeps on the earth—so that they may abound on the earth, and be fuitful and multiply on the earth.' So Noah went out with his sons and his wife and his sons' wives. And every animal, every creeping thing, and every bird, everything that moves on the earth, went out of the ark by families. Then Noah built an altar to the Lord, and took of every clean animal, and of every clean bird, and offered burnt offerings on the altar. And when the Lord smelled the pleasing odour, the Lord said in his heart, 'I will never again curse the ground because of humankind, for the inclination of the human heart is evil from youth; nor will I ever again destroy every living creature as I have done. As long as the earth endures, seedtime and harvest, cold and heat, summer and winter, day and night, shall not cease.

Some years ago, when my small son first heard the story of Noah, he was shocked. 'That isn't our God, is it, Daddy?' In fact, the storyteller agrees. The point of the story comes at the end of the flood, as Noah offers worship to God. God decides that destruction is not the way to deal with human sinfulness.

So the tale of the great flood, one of many flood stories from that part of the world, becomes a parable of God's response to human sin. Whatever he decides to do about the evil inclination of humanity, he will not simply give up and wipe away his creation. As long as the earth lasts, God will send his rain upon the just and the unjust alike.

Of course, the problem remains of what is to be done. The answer will be much longer in the telling than the rejected possibility of destruction. It concerns the forging of a people with a special relationship with God; a people among whom God may walk in human form, and from whom will come the message of the God who takes the weight of human sin upon himself.

Pray

Father, give us a true appreciation of your love and forbearance, so that we too may offer you our worship as a pleasing sacrifice.

MM

John 17:1, 20–23 (JB)

Unity

Jesus raised his eyes to heaven and said... 'I pray not only for these, but for those also who through their words will believe in me. May they all be one. Father, may they be one in us, as you are in me and I am in you, so that the world may believe it was you who sent me. I have given them the glory you gave to me, that they may be one as we are one. With me in them and you in me, may they be so completely one that the world will realise that it was you who sent me and that I have loved them as much as you loved me.'

There are those who will tell you that in the New Testament period the church was a unified, dynamic force sharing a common faith, a common experience of the Spirit and a common vision. This pristine church swept through the Roman world, winning great numbers of converts, and if only we would allow God to restore that church today, we would see great things happen.

It's nonsense, of course. Why does John include this great prayer for unity amongst the future followers of Jesus? Because the churches for which he wrote were no strangers to division. A glance at the letters of John will show that.

Yet that very fact can give us grounds for hope. God did indeed do great things through the early church. But he did it through a church that was often divided in fellowship and doctrine, full of imperfect squabbling people, eager for their own group to gain power, and to ready to do down the opposition. God uses ordinary, fallible people to do great things. He has to. There aren't any other kind.

That means he can do great things with us too. So there is hope.

At the same time, the divisions of the church are a real hindrance to God. A church that shows itself as fragmented and argumentative is no great advert for the kingdom of God. So today pray for all who work for Christian unity, both at official and unofficial levels. Pray too for the unity that comes of love and understanding within the local congregation, so that, as Jesus prayed, those who see the unity of love will be drawn to the source of all love: God himself.

MM

Genesis 9:1–6 (NRSV)

Life and death

God blessed Noah and his sons, and said to them, 'Be fruitful and multiply and fill the earth. The fear and dread of you shall rest on every animal of the earth, and on every bird of the air, on everything that creeps on the ground, and on all the fish of the sea; into your hand they are delivered. Every moving thing that lives shall be food for you; and just as I gave you the green plants, I give you everything. Only, you shall not eat flesh with its life, that is, its blood. For your own lifeblood I will surely require a reckoning: from every animal I will require it and from human beings, each one for the blood of another, I will require a reckoning for human life. Whoever sheds the blood of a human, by a human shall that person's blood be shed; for in his own image God made humankind.

A new age now begins, the age in which we live. God's blessing of increase is repeated, but much else has changed. The animals which once came to Adam to be named now flee from man the hunter. The creation of which God said, 'It is good,' is no longer entirely good. There has been a breakdown in the order of creation.

God's giving of the animal world as human food recognizes this dysfunction in creation. Things are not as they were, and there is no possibility of a return to Eden. The problem of sin has not been dealt with. Yet even though God acknowledges the new way of things, there are limits to human rapaciousness which must be recognized. Even though humans may now eat animals, they must recognize God as the ultimate giver, the source of life. The true power of life and death still lies with God, and human treatment of creation must still recognize this. Responsibility to the creator has not ended.

This is even more the case in the matter of human life. Humans are not simply smarter and faster carnivores. They share the image of God, and a possibility of a unique relationship with him. So murder is still prohibited—it is not simply another form of hunting. For us the twofold message is clear. We still have a responsibility to God for how we treat our world; human failings are no excuse. And people are still to be valued as the unique creation of God, the object of his love and his salvation.

Pray

Open our eyes, Lord to see the world as your gift, and to know the limits of our own power.

MM

Genesis 9:8–15 (NRSV)

Whenever you see a rainbow

Then God said to Noah... 'As for me, I am establishing my covenant with you and your descendants after you, and with every living creature that is with you... as many as came out of the ark. I establish my covenant with you, that never again... shall there be a flood to destroy the earth.' God said, 'This is the sign of the covenant which I make between me and you and every living creature that is with you, for all future generations. I have set my bow in the clouds, and it shall be a sign of the covenant between me and the earth. When I bring clouds over the earth, and the bow is seen in the clouds I will remember my covenant that is between me and you and every living creature of all flesh; and the waters shall never again become a flood to destroy all flesh....'

What sort of God do we believe in? It's a fair question, as we tend to shape God in the image which best suits us. In this passage we are given the basic ground rules for our picture of God.

In the Bible, God makes several covenants, or agreements, with people. He makes one with Abraham, and later with Abraham's descendants at Mount Sinai. He makes a covenant with David and his descendants, and in Jesus rewrites the old covenants to include all who put their faith in Christ.

With the covenant idea comes the declaration of God's faithfulness; he can be trusted to keep his word and to do as he has said. Today's reading is the first mention of the covenant term in the Old Testament, and it is a covenant with all of creation. God will never destroy it, no matter how great the provocation.

So when we speak of God, the basic idea is one of a God who is trustworthy and who cares for his creatures. The idea of the love of God is therefore stated at the very beginning. How that love will work out is the story of the rest of the Bible. That story ends with the remaking of creation which we see in the book of Revelation, where God (surrounded by the rainbow of his promise to Noah—Revelation 4:3) keeps his promise to creation by bringing about a new heaven and earth which will last for ever (Revelation 21:1).

Pray

Father, thank you for your faithful love, which leads to our salvation and the remaking of all that is.

MM

Genesis 9:20–27 (NRSV)

The morning after

Noah, a man of the soil, was the first to plant a vineyard. He drank some of the wine and became drunk, and he lay uncovered in his tent. And Ham, the father of Canaan, saw the nakedness of his father, and told his two brothers outside. Then Shem and Japheth took a garment, laid it on both their shoulders, and walked backwards and covered the nakedness of their father; their faces were turned away, and they did not see their father's nakedness. When Noah awoke from his wine and knew what his youngest son had done to him, he said, 'Cursed be Canaan; lowest of slaves shall he be to his brothers.' He also said, 'Blessed by the Lord my God be Shem; and let Canaan be his slave. May God grant space for Japheth, and let him live in the tents of Shem; and let Canaan be his slave.'

Noah's reaction may seem a bit strong to us, and his curse on Canaan, who after all was not even involved, is particularly unfair. But the story is a legend in which the nations and races are seen as being characterized by the nature of their traditional ancestors. Ham, who has no regard for his father's dignity (and perhaps sniggers at his nakedness) becomes a symbol for the Canaanites who posed a threat to the religion of Israel by the seductiveness of their fertility cults. Nakedness (and much more besides) played a prominent part in Canaanite worship.

The main point for us, though, is that the flood has not wiped out sin. We cannot be sure whether or not Noah was to blame for his drunkenness. He probably was not, if he had just discovered wine, and with it its intoxicating effects. However, the response of Ham is bad enough. In a society which placed great emphasis on respect for one's father, his dishonouring of Noah was serious stuff.

As long as human beings are permitted to survive (and God has now committed himself to this), then sin will survive too. So once again we see that if destruction is not the way to deal with it, another must be found. And so, from the line of Shem, God chooses a people, and from that people comes a saviour....

Pray

Father, thank you for the love and foresight which combine in the coming of Jesus to save us.

MM

Genesis 11:1–9 (NRSV)

Babble

Now the whole earth had one language... And... they came upon a plain in the land of Shinar and settled there. And they said... 'Come let us make bricks, and burn them thoroughly.' ... Then they said, 'Come, let us build ourselves a city, and a tower with its top in the heavens, and let us make a name for ourselves; otherwise we shall be scattered abroad upon the face of the whole earth.' The Lord came down to see the city and the tower, which mortals had built. And the Lord said, 'Look, they are one people, and they have all one language; and this only the beginning of what they will do; nothing that they propose to do now will be impossible for them. Come, let us go down, and confuse their language there...' So the Lord scattered them abroad from there over the face of all the earth, and they left off building the city. Therefore it was called Babel, because there the Lord confused the language of all the earth...

The last story in the opening section of Genesis is a timeless one. It is set in no particular relation to what has gone before, and does not involve any of the named descendants of Noah. Yet it sums up the theme of the first eleven chapters of the book. The tale is set against the background of ancient Babylon (Babel), with its temple-towers, or ziggurats: symbols of ancient piety which were the cathedrals of Babylon. On the surface, the story is meant to answer questions such as, why are there many nations and languages? and where does the name Babel come from? (In Accadian, the language of Babylon, the name means 'gate of god', but the Hebrew writer makes it a pun on 'balal', to confuse.) The real meaning of the story is more profound, however. The tower symbolizes the human quest for self-aggrandizement and security apart from God. But the end result is exactly what the city and its tower were meant to forestall, for apart from God there can be no security. Once again we see the theme of the human quest for self-fulfilment failing, because only in relation to God can there be true humanity. Human beings are created for God and by God and only there can they find true satisfaction.

Meditate

You have made us for yourself, O God, and our hearts are restless till they find their rest in you.

St Augustine of Hippo

MM

Genesis 12:1–4 (NRSV)

Faith

Now the Lord said to Abram, 'Go from your country and your kindred and your father's house to the land that I will show you. I will make of you a great nation, and I will bless you, and make your name great, so that you will be a blessing. I will bless those who bless you, and the one who curses you I will curse; and in you all the families of the earth shall be blessed.' So Abram went, as the Lord had told him; and Lot went with him. Abram was seventy-five years old when he departed from Haran.

Chapter 12 marks a new phase in the book of Genesis. We move out of the realm of myth into history. The story of Abram and his wife, Sarai, and their relatives and dependants, is set against the great migrations of peoples through Mesopotamia in the Bronze Age. How much is legend, and how much fact, is a matter that can never truly be settled. But we are definitely in the time of real people and real events.

The story hinges on one crucial factor—Abram's faith. He hears God speaking to him with a staggering promise; and on the basis of that he sets off to a distant land.

We often think of the great figures of the Bible as people who encountered God in a different way from us. If only we had their faith, if only we could hear the voice of God as clearly as they did, then we too would be great saints. But we are mere mortals, unsure of what is the will of God and what is wishful (or masochistic) thinking.

Yet we are not told that Abram heard God any more clearly than we do. The tale is told with the advantage of hindsight, and from there, even we can speak confidently of what God has said and done to us. It is at the actual time of decision that things are difficult. Abram's decision is to put his faith in the mysteriously different God who has singled him out, and to obey.

Such obedience is not easy. We often hear of the need for a 'step of faith'. We are often told that faith is about taking risks. What we are not so often reminded of, save by bitter experience, is that risks do not always work out. Steps into the dark sometimes lead us to land flat on our faces. But if we do not take the step, we get nowhere. Abram took it, and was blessed.

Pray

Father, give us faith to trust you, courage to put faith into action, and discernment to know when you are speaking to us.

MM

Genesis 12:10–13 (NRSV)

Deceit

Now there was a famine in the land. So Abram went down to Egypt to reside there as an alien, for the famine was severe in the land. When he was about to enter Egypt, he said to his wife Sarai, 'I know well that you are a woman beautiful in appearance; and when the Egyptians see you, they will say, 'This is his wife'; then they will kill me, but they will let you live. Say you are my sister, so that it may go well with me because of you, and that my life may be spared on your account.'

Faith is all very well, but we have to live in the real world. You've probably heard comments like that. Of course you have. In fact, if truth be told, we've almost all made them at some time. Not, perhaps, out loud, so that we can hear what we are really saying, but quietly, in our secret thoughts, stifling any actual full-blown decision but just letting ourselves follow a course that is unworthy, deceitful or cowardly.

Abram has travelled through Canaan, where God has promised to give that land to his descendants. But promises are all very well when one is secure and wealthy. Famine changes all that, and Abram must throw himself on the mercy of the Egyptians. Surely they will kill him to get the lovely Sarai. So he passes her off as available to be a concubine for Pharaoh (and gets a good deal out of the bargain). We're not told what Sarai thought of all this.

God, though, is not pleased. And neither is Pharaoh. When he finds out (by being afflicted with plagues from

God!) he sends Abram packing.

Abram has made two mistakes. Firstly, he has allowed fear to paint the Egyptians as monsters. In fact they are not. 'Why didn't you just say she was your wife?' asks Pharaoh. Abram does not say, 'Because fear crippled my judgment and destroyed my faith.' But he could have.

Secondly, Abram has underestimated God. Not by failing to believe God would keep him safe. Safety is not a divine promise. He has failed to realize that the God he serves demands integrity and holiness. God is not served by lying and cheating. His demand is for truth, and the faith to know that truth will be honoured by God.

Pray

Father, give me the faith to trust you when I am afraid, and to know that you are with me all the more at such times.

MM

Isaiah 50:4–6 (RSV)

Listening speaker

The Lord God has given me the tongue of those who are taught, that I may know how to sustain with a word him that is weary. Morning by morning he wakens, he wakens my ear to hear as those who are taught. The Lord God has opened my ear, and I was not rebellious, I turned not backward. I gave my back to the smiters, and my cheeks to those who pulled out the beard; I hid not my face from shame and spitting.

We think of the prophets as those who were (and are) called to speak the words of God. They come to call rebels to repentance and sinners to forgiveness. They announce the judgment of God, and proclaim his salvation. First and foremost they are speakers.

The prophet who wrote the second great section of the book of Isaiah (known as 'Isaiah of the Exile') was indeed a great speaker. It is in Isaiah chapters 40–55 that Israel's prophetic tradition reaches its peak. Yet the prophet seems not to have seen his first task as speaking out. Instead, it was listening.

Before he uses his tongue it must be taught; his ear must be wakened, and opened by God. The prophet is first and foremost a listener—a listener to God.

It may seem obvious, but the temptation to speak one's own words, to express one's own prejudices, hopes and fears, is often overwhelming. To speak the words of God alone takes careful listening indeed. So how did this prophet listen to God?

We might suppose he heard the divine voice directly, and maybe he did. But a reading of his words shows scores of references to the Psalms, to the Law of Moses, to earlier prophets. This was a man who read and reflected on scripture. If he heard the voice of God anywhere, it was in the words of his Bible, read, thought about and prayed over. And it was these words of God, reworked for a new time, which burst unstoppably out of the prophet, to challenge, reassure and provide direction to his despairing people.

So today, when we hear the scriptures read, don't develop a sudden interest in church windows. Listen, and hear the word of God, that we too may speak it to others.

MM

John 20:15 (RSV)

The search

'Sir, if you have carried him away, tell me where you have laid him and I will take him away.'

There she was standing in the garden weeping alone. Less than three years previously she had known what it was to be possessed by seven demons, borne the label 'prostitute', and the scorn of many wagging tongues. This woman knew she was a sinner.

But what brought her to the garden was not her past life but her recent years of repentance and faith. Faith in a man she had watched die on a cross and whose body she had now come to anoint in his burial chamber. That chamber was empty, the body gone, and Mary of Magdala turned weeping from the tomb's entrance to entreat the gardener. Even in disappointment and grief Mary Magdalene was eager to show her love and devotion by continuing her duties. But she did not know to whom she spoke. This was no gardener. She did not know his name, but he knew hers, 'Mary', he whispered and she had no further doubt as to his identity. 'Rab-boni!' (teacher) she cried, and her weeping turned to tears of joy. If we really knew his name as he knows ours we would know he is truly Lord. We would not confuse him with the gardener, or the false Christs of our own making that are concealed within our material greed or our deeply cherished ambitions.

He affirms for each of us this day, 'Behold the former things have come to pass' (Isaiah 42:9). Watch out! He is in control and things will change—if we will let him change them from within us. To commit our lives to him is also to recognize the need to be re-made.

Despite three years of learning from Jesus, it was still an immense shock to Mary when she was confronted with the resurrected Christ. Wherever we have searched for him in the past, hear the words again—'He's not here, he is risen.'

Re-creation starts with the willingness to be surprised by a living God.

Prayer

Lord, I want to love you. I need you. If I hold anything back my re-creation is incomplete. New birth is painful. Saviour I'm scared of all that pushing and lunging through the birth channel, all that struggling to be free. Creator, touch me in your womb and grant me safe passage towards daylight, and breath of life. I will not fear to open my lungs to the weeping if you hold me, a newborn, tight within your arms. Amen.

HM

Luke 10:40 (RSV)

The distractions

But Martha was distracted with much serving... and said, 'Lord, do you not care that my sister has left me to serve alone?'

I never could make pavlova the way I like it, crisp with meringue and not soggy with marshmallow. My sister always turns out great pavlovas every time, a triumph at family celebrations.

On reflection I used to wonder if Mary was patiently waiting for a taste of her sister's cooking as she sat enthralled at Jesus' feet soaking up his teaching. If so 'big sis' wasn't taking it as any compliment.

Martha appeared to be doing all the right things, endeavouring to meet the master's needs by utilizing her own particular gifts. The trouble was, Martha was distracted. Service itself was becoming all-consuming, at the expense of the master she sought to feed. She also became jealous of her sister's tradition-busting action of taking the place of pupil at the feet of Jesus while he was teaching, a position which, in the culture of the day, was reserved for the male student of a rabbi. In this profession, such tutelage often designated the student as one who follows in the steps of the teacher.

I would imagine that Jesus probably surprised both sisters when he replied, 'Mary has chosen the good portion, which shall not be taken away from her' (verse 42).

The Bible doesn't tell us what hap-pened then. I like to think that Mary had enough graciousness to get up and check the oven temperature and I imagine that Jesus would not have stopped Martha if she had knelt at his feet in her place. Whatever happened I expect that the two women learnt an important lesson about not turning service to the saviour into some kind of competitive drive for power. This lesson could well be heeded by all servants of his church of whatever generation or gender. New wine into old wineskins won't go. Something has to give. Far better to burst our old suppositions, prejudices and man-made traditions than to spill the precious contents of salvation onto the concrete ground of our own pride.

Jesus challenges us to be willing to be reshaped into new vessels, so that both the contents and the container are preserved (Matthew 9:17).

Prayer

Lord, remake me, all the way through to my behaviour and prejudices. I don't want to spill a drop of your precious contents. If this old container is too porous, change me right out to the skin. Amen.

HM

Revelation 21:5 (RSV)

Totality

And he who sat upon the throne said, 'Behold I make all things new.'

In a modern age, and a modern church, there can be the temptation to confine all discussion of re-creation to the realm of spirituality and the domain of the soul. Compartmentalizing the aspects of our own being, the soul gets taken out on Sunday for a quick 'polish' of the halo and is returned to storage in the cardboard box under the bed for the rest of the week. On Monday out comes the box marked 'intellect' for work or 'creativity' for relaxation and then there is 'body'—well perhaps for sport or for some other activity, considered to be equally unspiritual. In Mark 5:24–34 a woman was not afraid to bring to Jesus a part of her which most assuredly required re-creation. She was in no doubt that the needs of body, mind and soul were all one to him within his caring love. 'If I touch even his garments,' she said, 'I shall be made well.' (Mark 5:28) Having suffered for twelve years, this woman could not expect the modern treatment of a hysterectomy. Haemorrhage, accompanied by the ritual slur of being branded permanently unclean in accordance with the orthodox tradition of her culture, ensured that the dying was slow.

Ashamed to approach Jesus openly in her state of ritual impurity she humbly touched the edge of his garment under cover of the moving crowd. It was enough.

The God who makes all things new does not keep bodies, minds and spirits in separate boxes below the bed. The woman was cured—and Jesus knew it by the power that had been drained from him by virtue of her faith.

In Romans 8:22–23, St Paul, in painting a life-affirming picture, chose the image of a woman in childbirth awaiting the new life to be created. And he equates just such a struggle of groaning and travail to the entire planet—body, mind and soul; environment, power structures; creativity and spirituality. All endure labour pains to cooperate in the will of the creator God towards re-creation. Much effort is required to seek out and touch the hem of that garment in the crowd.

Prayer

Creator God, help me to bear these pangs of new birth. Be both instigator and midwife of the new life you wish to bring into fruition in me. Grant me a vision of spiritual adulthood. Hone my soul to maturity in the artistic workshop of your unfettered love. Please be tender with my body, Lord, it is such a mortal thing. Amen.

HM

2 Corinthians 5:16–17 (RSV)

Honestly yours

From now on, therefore, we regard no one from a human point of view; even though we once regarded Christ from a human point of view, we regard him thus no longer. Therefore if anyone is in Christ, he is a new creation; the old has passed away, behold, the new has come.

Read John 4:1–30. What a shock for the disciples when they arrived at the well in Samaria to meet up with Jesus and found him talking to a strange woman. It just wasn't the done thing and a Samaritan woman at that. 'For Jews have no dealings with Samarians' (John 4:9).

Here was more cultural conflict, more religious taboo for Jesus to break. I can imagine the conversation amongst the disciples:

'Honestly, we go to do a bit of shopping and come back to find *this*!' 'You'd think he'd be able to resist talking to a Samaritan!' 'By the look of her, I dare say she forced her company onto him.' 'But what was he thinking of, talking to a woman?' 'Move closer, can you hear what they're saying?' 'Yes, I think it's about—oh my goodness, he's talking about Jacob and salvation and...' '*Theology*! You can't be seriously suggesting that the master is discussing theology with a woman—a Samaritan woman, and look how she's dressed. I'd say her morals would be more than a little suspect.' 'Look out, here he comes.' 'Hello Jesus, every-

thing all right?' 'Thank you, yes, did you get the food?' 'Here it is, and I see you've drawn some water.' 'That lady over there drew it for me when I asked her.' '*You asked her!*' 'I was thirsty, but not quite as thirsty as she turned out to be. Peter, lay a cloth on the grass and let's invite her over to share our food, eh?'

Prayer

Dear Lord, thank you for seeing the inside of people before the outside slams the door on any possibility of a relationship. I'd like to do a spring clean on my interior before you sit down to eat and drink with me but I'm scared. No cleaning fluid I can imagine could tackle that job. You say a drink of the water you offer will do the cleansing. I believe you Lord, but might it do more? By the way, who else would you like me to invite to have tea with the two of us today? WHO was that you said?! Amen.

HM

Luke 19:8 (RSV)

Nothing withheld

Behold, Lord, the half of my goods I give to the poor, and if I have defrauded anyone of anything, I restore it fourfold.

Tree climbing was not the kind of activity which would normally have been associated with tax collectors in Jesus' day. They were usually considered by the locals to be odious, bureaucratic collaborators with the occupying forces and relegated, by all native citizens, to the top of the list to be ostracized. Add to all this the fact that Zacchaeus abused his civic occupation even further by creaming off a generous proportion of the taxes to line his own pockets and you have a picture of a little man not generally welcome to share 'crowd space' with the cheering Jews straining to see Jesus on the road. Yet Jesus stopped below this tree and announced his intention to let Zacchaeus be host to the Son of God, over tea.

The Bible does not relate the full conversation but the upshot was that Zacchaeus experienced a change of heart that not only remade him spiritually, but led to his giving back to all his victims, not twice as much as they'd been cheated, but fourfold of what he had embezzled from them, and that was after he had given half of all his worldly goods to the poor.

We glibly pray for re-creation and sincerely desire the Lord's touch on our lives to cleanse, renew and remould us into the shape which God originally designed us to be. But if we do not do so with a certain amount of trepidation then we have not fully understood just how much God is prepared to see us changed.

He will not take from us what we truly need but he is likely to strip us of a great deal of what we once believed were needs and can only later redefine as mere greed.

God wants only the best for us. The difficulty is that God's definition of 'best' and our definition can differ, and it can take a lot of tree climbing and numerous cut knees and elbows on our part before we catch the vision from a great height.

Prayer

Dear Lord, give me insight into my own soul and behaviour, in the light of what it should be. I know I cannot be perfect until heaven, but Lord, give me the courage not to wait until then before I make an effort towards holiness. I'd look a bit silly in a halo but 'right-ness-ness' is the least I can strive towards in gratitude to you. Help me make a start. Amen.

HM

Veils removed

And we all with unveiled face, beholding the glory of the Lord, are being changed into his likeness from one degree of glory to another; for this comes from the Lord who is the Spirit.

When Jesus turns and looks Peter in the eye as the cock crowed for the third time both men's faces were clearly visible—no veils. Perhaps that is why Peter 'went out and wept bitterly' (Luke 22:62).

Paul's teaching in 2 Corinthians refers to Moses veiling his face to shield the waiting Israelites from the last glimpse of radiance of God's glory after receiving the ten commandments, and it highlights the dual respect and shame which results from a direct encounter with the living God.

Paul assures us we can be 'bold' and come to the father with 'unveiled faces' as a direct result of Christ's action on the cross and of his subsequent resurrection. All veils are removed including the one in the temple which was torn from top to bottom as Christ sacrificed his life to pay the cost of our salvation.

We need not fear the direct gaze of a loving father. Yet we cannot hide our own eyes as we meet the gaze of Jesus whom we betray every time we act in any way other than love.

Peter walked from that courtyard not knowing if he would ever be forgiven. He ran to the tomb to find it empty. It was later by the sea when, out fishing, he caught nothing, and a stranger on the beach shouted to the boatmen to cast their nets on the other side. The catch was so great they could not haul it in. Peter—normally the impulsive, brash, headstrong leader—took time to put on his clothes before plunging into the sea to meet the stranger. Already his self-esteem had taken a battering. Already 'from one degree to another', he was being remade.

Then came Jesus' threefold question, 'Do you love me?', and the threefold commission to carry on the work he had previously entrusted to him.

By many 'degrees' Peter was transformed into the rock upon whom Christ would build his church.

Prayer

Lord, maybe this re-creation business is not so much the passive hibernation of caterpillar to butterfly as the painful, unexpected, eye-to-eye battle in the mirror when we recognize to what degree we still must submit, in order to be refashioned in the likeness of Christ. Amen.

HM

Romans 6:4 (RSV)

Feeling the burn

We were buried therefore with him (Christ) by baptism into death, so that as Christ was raised from the dead by the glory of the Father, we too might walk in newness of life.

When Paul wrote these words I wonder what particular visual image he had in mind to illustrate his own particular 'baptism into death'. It could have been a number of emotional experiences. There was certainly an abundance of choice, considering the long list of hardships, persecutions, and thorns in the flesh to which he had been subjected, but none of them could contend with that day on the road to Damascus when he submitted completely to the will of a sovereign God. For his obedience he remained blind for three days neither eating nor drinking. His deliverance from this dark tomb was dependent upon another servant of God, Ananias, obeying the Lord's command to go and heal the man whose reputation identified him as nothing but a threat and danger to Ananias himself. Yet he obeyed the command, took the risk and allowed himself to be used to restore the sight of the great missionary to the Gentiles.

Why the three dark days for Paul? The Lord himself gave the clue to Ananias; 'I will show him how much he must suffer for the sake of my name'. Do we preach too cosy a gospel in the twentieth century? In these days of Western greed and material comfort,

of instant credit, the myth of lottery happiness, of disposable marriage and superficial relationships, and of designer churches with individually tailored worship, have we forgotten to prepare the new convert for the cost of discipleship?

Paul, the first century's 'Mr Motivator', taught of running the race with effort, stamina and determination and he knew what he was talking about. In a nation of health fanatics, have we lost the spiritual concept of 'feeling the burn'.

Most of us, as followers of Jesus, long to have our 'rough edges' rubbed off, but few of us want to feel the sandpaper on our skin. Thankfully we are in the hands of a carpenter who knows how to treat both hard and soft wood in his loving fingers. However, 'newness of life' requires a new person to live it. Recreation does not happen overnight and cannot happen without both our co-operation and our perspiration.

Prayer

Lord Jesus, please don't use a mallet, but use whatever it takes to shape me into your likeness.

HM

Exodus 20:9–10 (RSV)

No waste in rest

Six days you shall labour and do all your work; but the seventh day is a sabbath to the Lord your God; in it you shall not do any work.

When an actor cannot find employment he says he is 'resting'. Rest is not necessarily recreation, especially if it is the enforced rest of unemployment. To experience true recreation, we must make peace with our resting. Embrace it, welcome it, apply discipline to it and most of all, discover what it is not. Embracing rest is easier when I remember that to do so is to follow the example of God himself; 'so God blessed the seventh day and hallowed it, because on it God rested from all his work which he had done in creation' (Genesis 2:3).

Wouldn't it be great to know how God spent his rest? Unfortunately we are told only that he refrained from creating for that period of time. It seems essential to all life, even divine life, to break up activity with rest periods. I cannot imagine God being 'tired', though I believe he understands exhaustion from knowing this experience in the life of Jesus. Rest, therefore, is not merely a muscular relaxation exercise. God is no 'couch potato'.

Sabbath observance requires a setting aside of normal weekday pressures and drives. It engages a conscious awareness of a horizon far beyond the confines of our own petty problems and agendas. It covenants time for him. I remember my niece, who is a grown teenager now, being angry with her grandmother when she was little. One day when Julie had been particularly high-spirited my Mum took her out to the garden and made her stand still suggesting she 'listen to the silence'. Long afterwards we were all enjoying a day at the seaside when the child did something naughty and before Mum could say a word she directed a guilty look at her grandmother and hotly announced, 'No I will *not* listen to the silence!' The poor infant had quickly associated the exercise of standing still as being some kind of punishment.

God waits for us to recognize that rest is not punishment, nor is sabbath observance a punitive Old Testament exercise. To experience true recreation we must learn how to rest.

Prayer

Dear Father, I have to keep going all the time. Maybe I need the adrenalin, or the praise, or perhaps, if I stood still I might hear something in the silence. Please give me courage to stand still long enough to 'listen to the silence'.
Amen.

HM

Philippians 4:6 (RSV)

Worry wastes life

Have no anxiety about anything, but in everything by prayer and supplication with thanksgiving, let your requests be made known to God. And the peace of God, which passes all understanding, will keep your hearts and minds in Christ Jesus.

Nothing prevents recreation like worry. We have all been there. You just get settled on the beach or in front of the TV, or driving out into the country you stop for a picnic, and just as your mind begins to switch off from the problems at home in shoots that other thought. It usually begins, 'What if...'

What if the car doesn't pass its MOT next week? What if I'm made redundant? What if that wee lump isn't innocent? Trying to say to someone, 'don't worry', is tantamount to saying, 'stop breathing'. A certain amount of worry is vital to our survival on earth. It is the spur that often galvanizes us into action. Without it would we look both ways before crossing the road, or make proper provision for our children's future, or have health checks? Taking reasonable precautions against possible future disasters seems pretty responsible behaviour. Yet Paul says, 'have no anxiety'. My best definition of anxiety is, 'living in a state of permanent uneasiness'. It is saying, 'No God, you are *not* in control, I am, and I'm scared because I can solve nothing.' Anxiety is about never really having thought through the concept of trust.

It's true that God will never do for us what we can do for ourselves. Neither will he leave us floundering when things are beyond us. He is trustworthy. No wonder Paul continued, 'with thanksgiving let your requests be made known to God'. Nothing combats anxiety like a thankful heart.

As a child with seven disabilities from birth, I would be lifted onto a very high sea wall by my Dad. He would give me a huge grin to encourage me to walk along it with the sheer drop to a raging sea below. I remember how I repeatedly enjoyed the experience, because not only did I love the sea, but also my father had a very tight hold of my hand as he walked along the harbour side of the wall. I still remember how I would stop at intervals and thank him with a squeeze of the hand. Relax, not because there is no deluge to come but because, in God's hands, we no longer need fear drowning.

Prayer

Dear Father,
Hold tight, here I come. Amen.

HM

Joshua 24:15 (RSV)

Only one master

And if you be unwilling to serve the Lord, choose this day whom you will serve... but as for me and my house, we will serve the Lord.

Re-creation is also about single-mindedness. Joshua, near the end of his life, was concerned to ensure the continued single-mindedness of Israel in its obedience to God's covenant. Surrounded as the people were with temptations and influences of a number of pagan cultures, this courageous leader, as Moses had done, again called them together to commit themselves. He challenged them to renew their vows to serve only Yahweh, not diluting that service by adhering to any outside pagan practice. They agreed, 'we also will serve the Lord, for he is our God' (verse 18). The basis for this covenanted service, was their gratitude for all that Yahweh had done for themselves and their fathers through past generations. Can you imagine that happening today? Imagine us all being called to one place in a huge wilderness (or in front of a television) and spoken to by a national spiritual leader.

'Citizens,' he might say, 'choose this day whom you will serve: the twentieth-century Western myth of happiness by acquisition of wealth, emotional self-gratification, individual egotistical reinforcement, elevation of your own family's rights at the expense of those of another; ... or the Lord.' It would be scary, wouldn't it?

Jesus warned us against trying to serve two masters; 'You cannot serve God and mammon' (Matthew 6:24). This is equally true of anything else that threatens to compete with our devotion to the Lord. To be reshaped in Christ's likeness God requires our full cooperation. Without a single-minded servant-heart such obedience to his will is both diluted and obstructed. 'Resting' in his love without anxiety, and enjoying the 'peace that passes understanding' is impossible to achieve if we are attempting to divide our loyalty and attention between many masters, ambitions and desires. Thankfully the people had not stopped listening to God's word through Moses and Joshua, and the result was a renewal of the covenant for the children of God. As for us? Well, that's another story; only we can decide.

Prayer

Dear God, this single-minded discipline takes a great deal of hard work. Have you seen the distractions around in this century, Lord? Help me identify and root out the things in my life that compete with you for my attention and devotion. I choose you Lord, because you first chose me.

HM

Matthew 6:33 (RSV)

Spiritual orienteering

Seek ye first his kingdom and his righteousness and all these things shall be yours as well.

It is wonderful how children can be a great source of spiritual truth, especially when they are not trying to be. When my niece was small she was in the car as her father drove the family on a holiday tour a long way from home. At one stage her Dad, looking puzzled, stopped to examine the map. 'What's wrong, Daddy?' she enquired. 'I've lost my bearings, Julie,' he replied. To which she chirped, 'I'll help you look for them Daddy, where did you leave them?'

We long for that attitude of re-creation that enables us to find our bearings amidst the maelstrom of pressures, stresses, temptations, confused responsibilities and misplaced loyalties which close in on us from the surrounding secular milieu. The problem is that most of us cannot remember where we left them.

Thankfully Jesus gave us a clue to what our attitude should be, when he was overheard in his own prayer to his Father in John 17:15; 'I am not asking you to take them out of the world, but I am asking you to protect them from the evil one' (NRSV).

It is both reassuring and challenging that choosing our priorities in life and in living is our responsibility. God trusts us with the task. If we have lost our bearings, it is chiefly up to us to find them again.

The good news is that it's never too late to look, and the Lord is constantly facilitating the search. Get out the old Sherlock Holmes magnifying glass though, for we might have to do some pretty intricate detective work to uncover the really valuable treasures hidden under all the years of frustration and failure, wounds and betrayal, not to mention hurt, of the past. Bitterness, unforgiveness, and hardened hearts are the best camouflage I know to disguise the priorities of his kingdom. Still, right-ness-ness (right-eousness) soon wipes the disguises away and lets us get things straight again, if we really want to seek the kingdom above all else.

Prayer

Dear Lord, I've only got one shot at this life business. Time is precious, please don't let me waste it on non-essentials or just plain wrong essentials. You know what I need and I suspect that it is a good deal less than I want. Help me find my bearings and head me towards the kingdom. Amen.
HM

Colossians 4:2 (RSV)

Never quit!

Continue steadfastly in prayer, being watchful in it with thanksgiving...

Paul, writing from prison, emphasizes again one of the recurring motifs of his letters—praying with thanksgiving.

He is a captive, he is praying, he is thankful, and he asks for more prayer. Not to escape, but that more doors will open for him. Doors of opportunity to enable him to be a more effective witness to the word of God. At the end of the letter he adds a little human postscript as an afterthought: 'I, Paul, write this greeting with my own hand. Remember my fetters' (v. 18). With his own hand, was this the grounds for his thankfulness? No one knows for sure what Paul's 'thorn in the flesh' was. Many have speculated upon the nature of the physically disability that dogged him for a lifetime. Perhaps blindness or poor eyesight dating back to the Damascus Road experience, or something similar to Parkinson's disease which would have made it equally difficult to write.

Whatever the problem, he took great pride whenever he was able to add this little postscript, also in 1 Corinthians 16:21, 2 Thessalonians 3:17, and Galatians 6:11, 'see what large letters I am writing to you with my own hand'. I can bear personal testimony to the fact that, when someone carries a disability for a lifetime, those things which can be accomplished are treasured and valued with an intensity deepened each time there is a temporary loss and reinstatement of facility. It is a profound truth that what we have never lost we often do not know how to value.

Paul presents us with the definitive example of a completely re-created life. He wrote in his letter to the Philippians, 'I know how to be abased, and I know how to abound, in any and all circumstances; I have learned the secret of facing plenty and hunger, abundance and want. I can do all things in him who strengthen me' (Philippians 4:12–13). A spirit of true recreation like his springs from an abiding attitude of contentment. If we have not cultivated that art we will never be truly at rest.

Prayer

Dear Father, did I ever tell you how much I appreciated your answer to my last prayer? Amen.

P.S. Paul says, 'remember my fetters', a human plea for prayer and sympathy from a giant of the Church, all the more poignant in the rare occasion of its usage. Please remember to pray for those in all kinds of bondage, remembering that not all prison bars are visible to the naked eye.
HM

2 Timothy 3:16 (RSV)

The hardest word

All scripture is inspired by God and profitable for teaching, for reproof, for correction, and for training in righteousness, that the man of God may be complete, equipped for every good work.

Listening to God by understanding what the Bible teaches is the first step in dealing with guilt—though our conscience within often plays a part prior to scripture itself.

How many of us decide to spring-clean just before going on holiday? How many rush to clear our desk work, or tidy the garden, or visit that elderly cousin we haven't attended for years, just before we concentrate on packing the case for our well-earned annual break? Perhaps not everyone, but the large proportion of the population who do can testify to a great sense of satisfaction on holiday when the chores are done first. Maybe the secret lies in the term 'well-earned' break. It is almost as though we must give ourselves permission to enjoy the break by getting the onerous tasks completed before we go. We seek to 'earn' the holiday before we claim the prize.

Not feeling worthy to deserve these things is an underlying tenet of the human condition. Self-esteem is a complex matrix and the reasons for its absence are many, and often stem from childhood experiences. But as Christians we do ourselves a disservice if we ignore guilt as a stumbling block to recreation. The Bible helps us take guilt seriously. Jesus was never 'soft' on sin. 'Go and sin no more', he told the woman caught in the act of adultery, while at the same time forgiving her sins and setting her free from the threat of death by stoning. 'Your sins are forgiven you', he told the paralysed man let down through the roof to be healed. Only afterwards did Jesus tell the man to take up his bed and walk. There is a freedom to be enjoyed in recreation only after addressing the problem of guilt. According to many modern pop songs 'sorry' seems to be the hardest word to say, especially if God expects us to go and say sorry to the person we've made angry or to whom we have done wrong, or, worse still, to the person we consider has wronged us. Now that really would be taking forgiveness a bit far wouldn't it? How far, Lord? Seventy times seven, Peter.

Prayer

Lord, feed me with your word that I may obey your laws. Grant me recreation unsullied by the twinges of conscience. Thank you for your graciousness in listening and forgiving, whatever I've done. Amen.

HM

Philippians 4:4 (RSV)

Joy—it is a harvest word

Rejoice in the Lord always; again I will say, Rejoice.

It's that man again! St Paul, putting us to shame. You'd think he would have a decent moan now and again, just to make the rest of us feel a little better.

Mind you, rejoicing in the midst of imprisonment and persecution and thorns in the flesh and everything else a Christian must contend with, that sounds like a fully re-created person to me, totally the master of his circumstances. Our master, Jesus Christ, has won against all Satan's negatives and the final victory is promised.

We are called to be offensive, not defensive, in Christian living and we find it hard to rejoice because we don't feel like winners. Well, we might never *feel* that we are winning, because part of the enemy's tactics are to blind us to all advances made.

Feelings are no good on a battlefield. They make soldiers either callous or cowards. Only by keeping an eye on the captain and pressing forward can we make headway. In the meantime battlefields are dodgy places to be. They are rough and dirty and the stench of blood is forever in the nostrils. Jesus never said it would be easy—he promised it would be possible.

If we wait for our feelings to catch up with where we are at present we will miss out on a great deal of celebration in this life. Paul never said 'rejoice when you feel like it'. He recommends that we rejoice now—and feel good later.

In gratitude, we learn to take God seriously and ourselves a little less so. In rejoicing, we learn to laugh at ourselves and our petty hurts and grievances. Not that they are petty to us—and thankfully not to God either—but maybe we need another trip to the funfair where we can stand in front of mirrors which show ourselves distorted into extreme fatness one minute and squeezed skinny the next. Laughing in relief at what we are not helps us to begin to address what we truly are.

We are children of the living God, loved and cared for and constantly forgiven, despite our own wilfulness and stupidity. And every moment the Saviour is gently working to remould and re-create us into his likeness so that we may experience true recreation. Now if that's not something to rejoice about—I don't know what is!

Prayer

Dear Lord, rest me in your love. Relax me in your service. Re-create me in your image until those around me know the refreshment of your personal touch upon their lives. Amen.

HM

New Daylight © BRF 1997

The Bible Reading Fellowship
Peter's Way, Sandy Lane West, Oxford, OX4 5HG
ISBN 0 7459 3528 1

Distributed in Australia by:
Albatross Books Pty Ltd, PO Box 320, Sutherland,
NSW 2232

Distributed in New Zealand by:
Scripture Union Wholesale, PO Box 760, Wellington

Distributed in South Africa by:
Struik Book Distributors, PO Box 193, Maitland 7405

Distributed in the USA by:
The Bible Reading Fellowship, PO Box M, Winter Park,
Florida 32790

Publications distributed to more than 60 countries

Cover photograph: Jon Arnold

Printed in Denmark

SUBSCRIPTIONS

☐ I would like to give a gift subscription (please complete both name and address sections below)

☐ I would like to take out a subscription myself (complete name and address details only once)

☐ Please send me details of 3- and 5-year subscriptions

This completed coupon should be sent with appropriate payment to BRF. Alternatively, please write to us quoting your name, address, the subscription you would like for either yourself or a friend (with their name and address), the start date and credit card number, expiry date and signature if paying by credit card.

Gift subscription name _____

Gift subscription address _____

_____ Postcode _____

Please send to the above, beginning with the May/September 1997 issue:

(please tick box)	UK	SURFACE	AIR MAIL
LIVEWIRES	☐ £12.00	☐ £13.50	☐ £15.00
GUIDELINES	☐ £9.30	☐ £10.50	☐ £12.90
NEW DAYLIGHT	☐ £9.30	☐ £10.50	☐ £12.90
NEW DAYLIGHT LARGE PRINT	☐ £15.00	☐ £18.60	☐ £21.00

Please complete the payment details below and send your coupon, with appropriate payment to: **The Bible Reading Fellowship, Peter's Way, Sandy Lane West, Oxford OX4 5HG**

Your name _____

Your address _____

_____ Postcode _____

Total enclosed £ _____ (cheques should be made payable to 'BRF')

Payment by cheque ☐ postal order ☐ Visa ☐ Mastercard ☐ Switch ☐

Card number: ☐☐☐☐ ☐☐☐☐ ☐☐☐☐ ☐☐☐☐

Expiry date of card: ☐☐☐☐   Issue number (Switch): ☐☐☐☐

Signature (essential if paying by credit/Switch card) _____

NB: BRF notes are also available from your local Christian bookshop.

ND0297   The Bible Reading Fellowship is a Registered Charity

BIBLE READING RESOURCES PACK

A pack of resources and ideas to help to promote Bible reading in your church is available from BRF. The pack which will be of use at any time during the year includes sample editions of the notes, magazine articles, leaflets about BRF Bible reading resources and much more. Unless you specify the month in which you would like the pack sent, we will send it immediately on receipt of your order. We greatly appreciate your donations towards the cost of producing the pack (without them we would not be able to make the pack available) and we welcome your comments about the contents of the pack and your ideas for future ones.

This coupon should be sent to:

The Bible Reading Fellowship
Peter's Way
Sandy Lane West
Oxford OX4 5HG

Name _____

Address _____

_____

_____ Postcode _____

Please send me _____ Bible Reading Resources Pack(s)

Please send the pack now/ in_____ (month).

I enclose a donation for £_____ towards the cost of the pack.

BRF PUBLICATIONS ORDER FORM

Please ensure that you complete and send off both sides of this order form.

Please send me the following book(s):

		Quantity	Price	Total
2526	Time to Change (H. Montefiore)		£6.99	
3516	Connecting with God (J. Levermore)		£5.99	
2522	Visions of Love (W. Sykes)		£10.99	
2591	Visions of Hope (W. Sykes)		£10.99	
2977	Visions of Glory (W. Sykes)		£9.99	
3098	Visions of Faith (W. Sykes)		£10.99	
3503	Visions of Grace (W. Sykes)		£11.99	
3509	The Jesus Prayer (S. Barrington-Ward)		£3.50	
3253	The Matthew Passion (J. Fenton)		£5.99	
3295	Livewires: Footsteps and Fingerprints (R. Sharples)		£3.50	
3296	Livewires: Families and Feelings (H. Butler)		£3.50	
3522	Livewires: Friends and Followers (S. Herbert)		£3.50	
3523	Livewires: Tiptoes and Fingertips (B. Ogden)		£3.50	
2821	People's Bible Commentary: Genesis (H. Wansbrough)		£5.99	
2824	People's Bible Commentary: Mark (R.T. France)		£7.99	
3281	People's Bible Commentary: Galatians (J. Fenton)		£4.99	
3510	The Unlocking (book) (A. Plass)		£5.99	
3512	The Unlocking (cassette) (A. Plass) (incl VAT)		£7.99	
3299	Forty Days with the Messiah (book) (D. Winter)		£5.99	
3542	Messiah (cassette) (D. Winter/S. Over) (incl VAT)		£8.99	
3544	Forty Days with the Messiah (pack) (D. Winter/S. Over) (incl VAT)		£13.99	
2825	Mark for Starters (D. Winter)		£2.99	
2523	Confirmed for Life (S. Brown/G. Reid)		£2.99	
2971	Feeding on God (S. Brown)		£2.99	
2990	Value Me (book) (S. Brown/P. Lawson Johnson)		£5.99	
2991	Value Me (pack) (S. Brown/P. Lawson Johnson) (incl VAT)		£13.98	
2598	Day by Day Volume 1 (various)		£10.99	
3250	Day by Day Volume 3 (various)		£10.99	

Total cost of books £ _____

Postage and packing (see over) £ _____

TOTAL £ _____

See over for payment details. All prices are correct at time of going to press, are subject to the prevailing rate of VAT and may be subject to change without prior warning.

NB: All BRF titles are also available from your local Christian bookshop.

ND0297   The Bible Reading Fellowship is a Registered Charity

PAYMENT DETAILS

Please complete the payment details below and send with appropriate payment and completed order form to:

The Bible Reading Fellowship,
Peter's Way,
Sandy Lane West,
Oxford OX4 5HG

Name _____

Address _____

_____

_____ Postcode _____

Total enclosed £ _____ (cheques should be made payable to 'BRF')

Payment by cheque ☐ postal order ☐ Visa ☐ Mastercard ☐ Switch ☐

Card number: ☐☐☐☐ ☐☐☐☐ ☐☐☐☐ ☐☐☐☐

Expiry date of card: ☐☐☐☐   Issue number (Switch): ☐☐☐☐

Signature (essential if paying by credit/Switch card) _____

POSTAGE AND PACKING CHARGES			
order value	UK	Europe	Surface	Air Mail
£6.00 & under	£1.25	£2.25	£2.25	£3.50
£6.01–£14.99	£3.00	£3.50	£4.50	£6.50
£15.00–£29.99	£4.00	£5.50	£7.50	£11.00
£30.00 & over	free	prices on request		

Alternatively you may wish to order books using the BRF telephone order hotline: 01865 748227